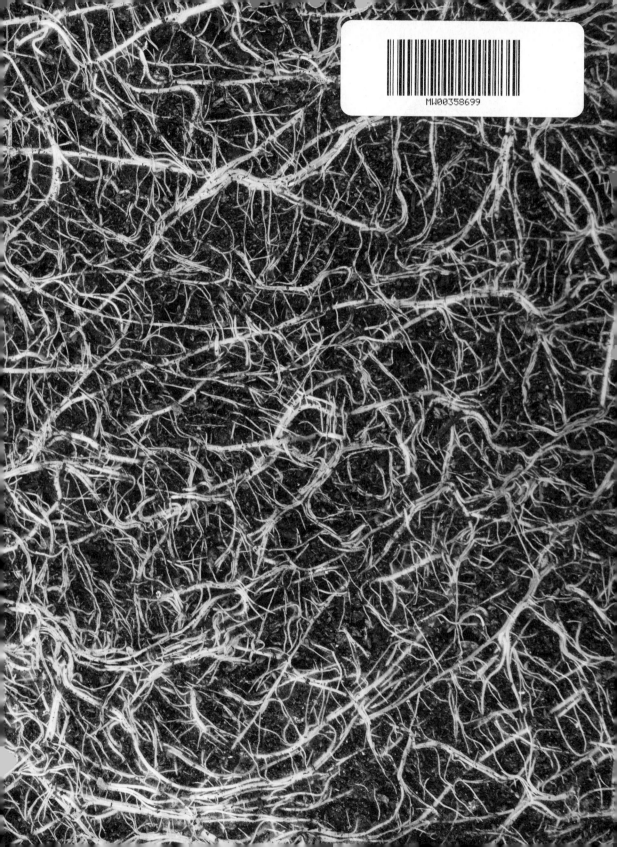

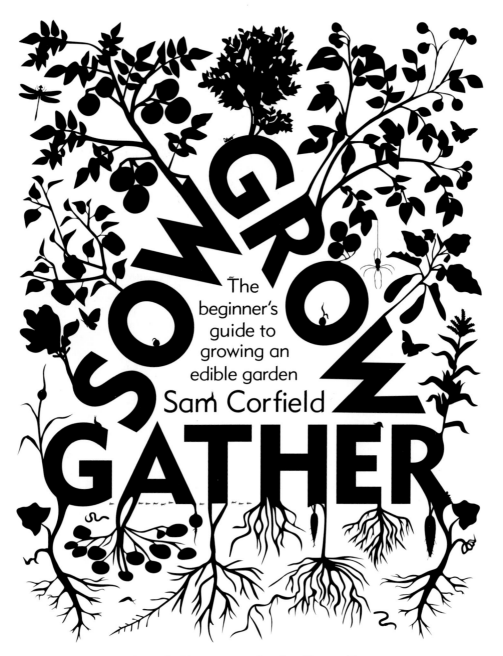

SOW GROW GATHER

The beginner's guide to growing an edible garden

Sam Corfield

Design & Photography by Dave Brown

Hardie Grant

QUADRILLE

Contents

Introduction

Hi. I'm Sam and I've ruined my serious horticultural career by posting photos of myself online… with vegetables. To be honest, it's not really ruined and, if anything, it's allowed me to get thousands more people from all walks of life interested in growing their own food.

Horticulture has been part of my life for as long as I can remember, but professionally I've been growing things for over 18 years. I began my working life at the world-renowned Lost Gardens of Heligan in the UK, and this helped me to learn continuously while constantly talking to visitors and offering advice. Back then, I was a slender, clean-shaven boy who dreamed of fitting slow cars with loud exhausts. In some ways, I haven't just been tied to just one industry, as horticulture leads to many other avenues like forestry, farming and conservation. After several years at Heligan, I found myself working in wildlife and, subsequently, spending several years as a cameraman for the BBC Natural History Unit. Following this, I moved to New Zealand for six months and became head gardener of a private garden. On my return, by chance, I became involved with creating a kitchen garden at my local pub, The Polgooth Inn in Cornwall, UK. Here, I really cultivated my skills in vegetable and beard growing and created a beautiful kitchen garden supplying fresh produce to the pub kitchen.

Gardening can be boring – I should know! I've lost several days of my life pulling weeds out of the ground in the rain, while humming teen pop songs. However, there is something special about growing plants – especially those you can eat. Gardening books don't need to be boring. They should be fun and light-hearted while still offering up all the main ingredients you need to grow a brilliant garden. Bringing humour to horticulture is something I enjoy and seems to be a really great way of getting everyone interested in growing their own food. Growing food in containers is something I've always done and I'm always recommending it to people. You don't need a large garden, a huge greenhouse or a beard. Just some soil, seeds and pots.

Just before we delve into the growing world of plants, you're probably thinking, why do I have to sow new plants each year?

Well, most of the edible plants that I talk about are 'annuals', which means they grow, reproduce and die all in one year. 'Perennial' plants, like strawberries, will effectively go through the same process as annuals but, instead of completely dying, they lose their leaves and die back before reappearing the following spring and starting the process all over again. You'll be uprooting lots of dead plants in winter, but this means you can prep your pots and beds and get very excited buying new seed varieties to grow next year.

Now go sow, grow, gather and just don't… muck it up!

What's in your toolbox?

When it comes to using basic equipment in your edible growing space, you don't always need to go and buy loads of fancy tools. There are actually tons of things around the house you can use, including those very helpful appendages called 'hands'. Here's my list of useful tools that will come in handy on your growing quest.

Bamboo canes

These are very important for creating supports and structures for your plants to climb up or lean on. Of course, you can use other sticks as supports, but bamboo canes are perfect for using with loads of different plants and if you look after them, they can last for years.

Dibber

This is a tool used for making holes in the compost when sowing or transplanting. You can buy a proper one, but I like to use pens and pencils, or even my finger, as they work just as well.

Hands

Yes, they are pretty useful and my number one tool. Use them as dibbers, shovels, mixers, sieves… the list is endless!

Secateurs

These are great for cutting back and trimming plants, as well as cutting string and twine. Most gardeners have them and there are some very fancy versions out there, but you just need a basic pair.

Seed dispenser

Not vital, but it can be really helpful for sowing those fiddly little seeds that you struggle to pick up with your fingers.

Sieve

You can use a sieve to create different grades of compost from the same bag. Fine, sieved compost is perfect for sowing your seeds, whereas the coarser stuff straight from the bag is great for potting on your seedlings.

String

I'm not talking about household string here, but garden string/twine, which has enough strength to hold up plants and tie your supports together. There are tons of options and you'll discover what works best for you by trying them out. I'm a fan of natural jute for most jobs.

Trowel

This is a must for digging holes and planting things out. You can get lots of different shapes, including a forked version.

Water containers

There are a lot of different options for watering your plants (which I mention in the next section), but as long as you have a basic watering can and a misting bottle, you'll be able to keep your plants happy.

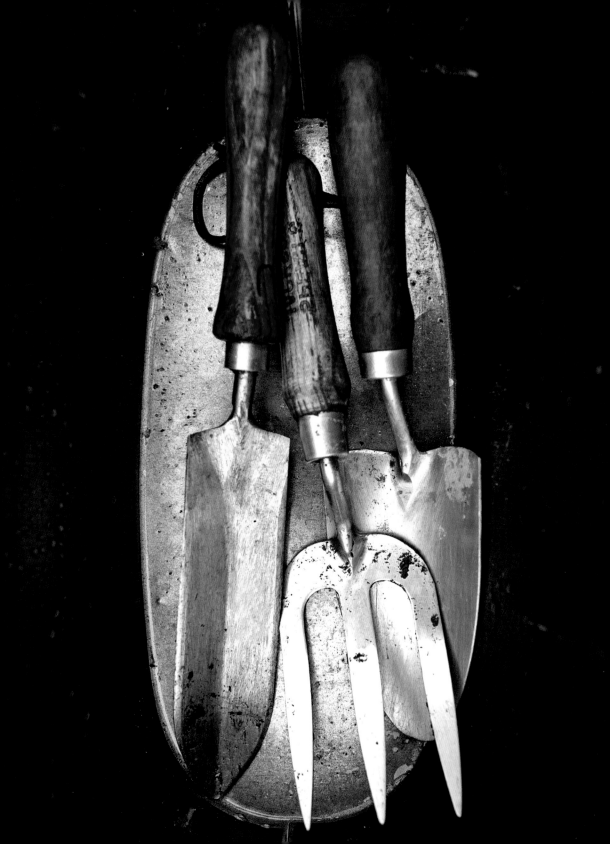

I wet my plants

"Look Sam, I know how to water a plant… I have a shower with it right?"

Wrong. There's a little more to it than just squirting a bit here and there every so often. So, what are the best methods when it comes to saving time and not pouring water down the drain? We all know that water is pretty important and when it comes to growing fruit and veg at home you want to make the most of it, especially if you've got lots of pots or raised beds, which can dry out faster than a Saharan puddle.

The three main things I bang on about when it comes to the wet stuff are:

Catch it – I don't mean using your hands! Make sure all your pots have trays under them so excess water can be caught and soaked up by the plant.

Less is better – You're not creating an aquarium, you want the soil to be damp rather than soaking wet.

Keep it regular – Try to water all your plants once or twice a day, first thing in the morning or last thing at night.

It might sound like I'm talking about bodily functions, but I promise these three things all work in harmony to keep your plants happy. So, if you water a moderate amount twice a day, you'll have less run off to catch and won't waste any water. Plants are living creatures and, with all living things, they just want to 'get it on', especially when they feel happy. If plants aren't happy, things can go awry. A great example is tomatoes; if you water them too much and not regularly, then the fruit can split and will lose flavour. If you give any plant too much or too little water, not only can it hinder their growth, it might also force them to reproduce too quickly and you'll be without any veg to get your chops round.

Watering seeds
Make sure your water isn't the temperature of the Arctic Circle as this will 'shock' the seeds. I prefer to water my seeds from above once I've sowed them using a spray bottle. This way you can create a humid atmosphere (humidity allows the seeds, and later foliage, to absorb moisture from the air and prevent them drying out) rather than soaking the soil too much. Remember, completely sodden soil can lower the temperature around your seeds and also encourage rot. Once the seeds have germinated, you should reduce or stop watering from above as this can promote fungus and other nasty bacteria. Instead, water from below in a tray (or similar) so that the soil can soak the liquid up from the bottom and encourage the roots to grow downwards.

Watering plants

Fully grown plants can be watered from above and below, but try to avoid standing water on the surface of the soil. You can do this by installing a tube pushed into the soil so that you can pour the water directly under the surface.

Watering equipment

Yes, those shiny rose-gold watering cans you see online are pretty, but they aren't actually all that practical – what we want is something that works. Bottles with holes drilled in the lid are great, watering cans (traditional, large-capacity metal or plastic watering cans built for watering, not looks), hand sprayers and water trays are all things you might want to consider using throughout the growing season. Now, I love a good hose, but I find them quite wasteful and when watering containers you can easily over-water the plants and wash precious nutrients out of the soil. It's always best to stick to more gentle methods.

Top tech

Technology is really important in the world of food production these days. Even growing-your-own has a few 'high-tech' options that are not only in regular use, but are also becoming much cheaper than they used to be. You can now buy timed watering systems with drippers and soakers that come on throughout the day and automatically water your plants, keeping them perfectly wet and giving you the spare time to brush your hair or take selfies with your melons! Self-watering systems obviously won't work for everyone's space, but if you're able to get one, they're a great option – I love using them.

I'm hungry

I'll try not to bore you with the scientific details, but I will tell you that the main ingredients that plants need to survive are nitrogen for foliage, phosphorus for roots, flowers and fruits, and potassium for all functions within the plant. These three elements are also known as NPK. This term is used to describe both natural and man-made fertilizers. If you're feeling low on energy, then you're probably not going to be in the mood for 'adult hugging', and the same applies for your fruit and veg plants. Plants need this balance of NPK so they have the energy to keep reproducing. But it's not always needed – sometimes there can be enough energy stored in the compost or soil that the plants are growing in to keep them happy.

There are a lot of options when it comes to feeding your plants. The types of feed are either in a solid or liquid form, and include various artificial liquid fertilizers, seaweed and lots of different animal dung, including chicken and horse to name but two.

If you really want to impress everyone with your vegetable growing wizardry, then you might want to make your own liquid feed. This can be done by soaking various plant leaves or certain old animal faeces in water until the nutrients leach out of them and form a tasty liquid feed – yummy! Try things like chicken or sheep droppings, horse manure or cow dung, stinging nettles, comfrey, banana peel or dock leaves. Pop that witches' hat on and crack out the cauldron while you mix up a liquid lunch! Always apply feeds to the soil surface and not on the foliage – unless it is specifically for foliage of course.

A note on hydroponics
Sure, it's traditionally associated with cannabis growing, but times are changing and hydroponics' companies are now selling some great bits of kit for the modern vegetable grower. These set-ups nourish plants with a feed and water mix in pots, but no soil, and produce huge plants and yields. These systems are readily available and aren't all that expensive for the small veg grower at home, so worth checking out.

Sowing seed

There are lots of different ways to sow seeds and everyone learns their own special tips and tricks over time. For me, small seeds like radish and kale can be really hard to handle when sowing into the individual cells of a seed module tray.

To make sowing them easier, I like to imagine I'm giving a quick tweak with my thumb and finger, just with a few seeds held between them. This works well when you're sowing seeds that are big enough to handle, but for really tiny seeds you might struggle. Do feel free to fumble away using your fingers, but you might benefit from getting a little seed dispenser to help you out. Don't be afraid to sow a little on the thick side as seedlings can always be removed or you can just embrace a thicker bush.

Now, after you've sown your heart out you have several options on where to let your seeds germinate, including in propagators, hot cupboards, sunny windowsills, etc. But the most important thing is that it is hot! Having good heat and humidity really helps your seeds germinate and stops any seed casings sticking to the seedlings and damaging them.

Propagators are great if you only have a few plants to germinate and they are fairly cheap to buy. If you want to recreate a humid propagator but don't have the real deal, then just use a small clear plastic bag placed over each pot. This will keep the humidity high and they can be removed once the seedlings have appeared.

I'm a big fan of soaking pulses – edible pulses like beans and peas. Soaking them before planting allows them not only to absorb lots of water, but also to germinate easily. I've had issues before with my friendly garden mouse eating his way through freshly sown peas and so allowing them to germinate out of the soil gives the plants a head start. Soak the seeds in between some kitchen paper for a couple of days or until you see the tap roots appear. Don't let them dry out!

Finally, there's no harm in cheating – I do it all the time. If you want to, you can skip the seeds and buy some plug plants online or from a local garden centre.

Talk dirt to me

Compost is all the same, right? Wrong! It's a bit like being asked to go and buy sugar. You get to the shop and then need to decide which type you need – granulated, muscovado, caster, icing or demerara?

In the world of soil and compost you can get all sorts of varieties and mixes and this can be pretty important when you're growing in pots and containers. Generally speaking, I stick with a multipurpose compost as it's a great all-rounder and, once sieved, is perfect for seed sowing as well. Sieving soil is a handy way to get a really fine grade of compost for those seedlings. It's probably best not to use your finest kitchen sieve – all you need is a garden sieve that you can shake over a bucket and allow the fine soil to fall into it. The soil we put into our containers provides our plants with nutrients throughout the season, so we need to ensure that there are enough nutrients in the compost to begin with.

Now, much like making a cake, you might need to add different ingredients to your compost. You might want to add a nutritional kick by using some horse manure (perfect for plants like potatoes, courgettes and pumpkins), or maybe add some vermiculite (a mineral) or perlite (a volcanic rock). Both occur naturally and provide great water retention, plus they aerate the soil – all plants love them. Whatever you add is entirely up to you and there are lots of different pre-made mixes or homemade 'recipes' out there (check out my Instagram @the_hairy_horticulturist for some muddy inspiration if making your own).

In the past, I've added man-made fertilizers but I now try to stick to decent composts, enriched with liquid feeds once the plants have established. Seed composts are available, but I find them too sandy to use so, as I mentioned above, try sieving multipurpose compost to get a fine tilth (a smooth, fine mix with no lumps – a bit like a dry cake mix).

Watch out for peat – it's not a guy who's decided to spell his name differently, I'm talking about peat bogs. Peat bogs are a super source of nutrients, but have been harvested over several decades for fuel and compost. The issue with this is that they have a lot of junk in their trunk – most of it is carbon – and as the peat bogs are harvested, this carbon is released into the atmosphere, which is bad for the planet. If you can find a peat-free compost, and it doesn't resemble a pile of wood chips, then use it. In the end, soil and soil health is very important and we should be caring for this black gold rather than destroying and abusing it.

I can't contain myself

Pots, bags, baskets, beds, boxes… No, I'm not moving house, I'm trying to decide what to plant my vegetables in. You might look at that list and think, what the muck? How do I know what to use? Well, the answer is to choose something you like, which is suitable for the type of plant you're growing and that works best for your space.

Plants can grow anywhere as long as there is enough light. This means you can grow them in pretty much any kind of container you can get your hands on, even if it's an old toilet, a bin, a tank or even your partner's favourite kitchen Tupperware! You can even plant directly into bags of compost.

Personally, I like to experiment all the time and usually end up planting my veggies in some sort of recycled or reclaimed container. If you want to invest in some new pots, containers or baskets, then go for it, just make sure they're of decent quality and are reusable. I'd recommend first heading to your nearest plant centre as they usually offer used pots for free, which I love diving into – beard-first – for a good rummage. You'll need pots and trays of various sizes, but always make sure you're giving your plant enough space to grow. I've indicated the size of pot you'll need for each of the plants in this book, but here's a little more detail on what to look for in a container.

The three main things you should consider when choosing a container:

Type
You can basically grow plants in any type of container, but if you're investing in new pots look for something durable and reusable like terracotta, concrete or toughened plastic. Where you can, reuse household items – toilet roll tubes are perfect for growing seedlings in and you can even grow plants in old bottles, guttering, wooden boxes or an old sink! If you have space, raised beds make a great home for your plants to thrive.

Size
As I've already said, you need to give those roots space to grow, so choose the size of your pots wisely, my young vegetable Jedi. Like a lot of things in life, bigger is better, but you've also got to work with the space you've got. No space is too small. If you only have a patio or even a window box to grow in, use containers that will fit that space and choose your plants accordingly. Also, keep in mind that you may want to move your plants or containers at some point and, therefore, having a giant container might be impractical. If you're growing plants indoors, consider the space they will take up and the way this might look – find spaces by doors and windows where you can squeeze in a pot here and there.

Like humans, pots come in various colours, shapes and sizes, but the most confusing thing is that some are measured in centimetres across the diameter of the top and some are measured by capacity in litres. Just to make it super confusing, I mention both in this book because you will encounter both on your vegetable quest, so you should learn to deal with it sooner rather than later.

Drainage

You need to ask yourself: do I want water running on the floor? Do I mind if my wall-mounted baskets dribble down my walls? The answer will most likely be, no thank you! Drainage is about making the perfect growing conditions for your plants. Most standard pots have holes in the bottom of them, which will provide adequate drainage, but you need to place trays underneath your pots to catch and retain any excess water. If you're using containers that don't have any drainage holes you will want to drill some holes in the bottom so that your soil doesn't become waterlogged, which will ultimately make your plants rot.

If you've got the space, then try building or buying some raised beds. I promise that you don't need a big plot to do this and it will optimize your growing space as well as helping to hold moisture in the compost.

I need some support

Now, although moral support is great for humans, it's not going to work on your melons. In the wild, plants can grow on other plants and use each other to hold on to and reach for the sky. Unfortunately for them, we tend to grow our plants in containers where there isn't anything else for them to climb up and so we need to provide some kind of support. As a child, I recall my father and grandfather each creating very neat geometric runner bean frames using bamboo canes. It seems everyone has a certain way of creating plant supports and no two ways are the same.

You've got endless options when it comes to choosing some support for your beans or cucumbers. Some popular options are natural or man-made string, which can be strung up and used to help support various plants. A helpful string method I was once shown works great for tomatoes and cucumbers, and involves getting each plant to self-anchor itself. When you plant your baby plants into their final growing space for the season, you make a loop at the end of a piece of string and then bury it under the plant as you're planting them out. As the plant grows, its roots grow into the loop and this holds it solid. All you have to do then is attach the other end of the string to a point above the plant and wrap the plant around the string as it grows.

Canes of all types and sizes are great as they can be joined together and provide something a bit more stable for your plants to grow up – try using bamboo, hazel and metal canes and see what works best for you. You can also utilize structures that you might already have at home, like placing plants underneath railings, handrails or archways. There's nothing better than a handrail covered with beautiful squashes, or cucumbers hanging from an archway. And again, try to reuse and recycle where possible – some of the more unusual types of support I've seen include stockings, children's play frames, old wire and fishing nets… be inventive and see where it gets you, but maybe avoid old underwear and stick to the basics first.

I like plants, but they're just too big!

I promise that you can grow edible plants in even the smallest of spaces – and this book will show you how. You have to learn to work with what you have, but if space is really at a premium, then you may want to focus your efforts on 'microgreens' or 'microleaves'.

For many years, these salad crops were only seen in high-end restaurants with celebrity chefs arranging them with tweezers as if they were a radioactive substance. They weren't radioactive, they were just expensive. Fortunately, this has slowly changed as people discovered how easy they are to grow at home. It might sound horrible, but I'm always describing microherbs as the 'veal of the vegetable world' as the principles are the same. We are essentially growing baby plants fast and then harvesting them at a really young age when they're still small – perfect for your small space.

Now, let's get down to business. Yes, they are very easy to nurture at home; you can easily grow them on a windowsill or under artificial grow lights. One of the main things I like about microleaves are the intense flavours and colours you get within a few days of sowing the seeds. You can sow them into soil or fibre matting, but I prefer to use compost as it is cheap and seems to work well at home.

There are lots of detailed guides online about how to grow microgreens, but I like to keep things simple. Sow a really thick layer of seeds in a seed tray or small pot, two-thirds filled with compost, cover with a little more compost and keep them

watered. Once they've appeared (four to twelve days – some microgreens grow faster than others) and have reached a height of around 5cm (2in) you can cut them off and eat them. Pretty simple right? Once you've decapitated them that's the end for these little plants, but simply repeat the steps above for another crop a couple of weeks later.

Even if you're limited to these mini edible plants, you've still got a huge choice of varieties from which to choose. You can grow the stunning pink amaranth, fresh pea shoots, nutty sunflowers, contentious coriander, basil, chives, chard, beetroot, mizuna. The list goes on, which is why you should dive in head-first and give these little fellas a try.

Problematic pests

Step away from my melons, hands off my cucumber, stop eating my cabbage!

These are all common things you'll hear in any garden around the world – why does everything want to eat your prized fruit and veg? Probably because they taste great and we share this world with lots of other creatures looking for plants to eat. This has always been an issue when growing crops and, traditionally, pests and diseases are killed with nasty chemicals, which isn't great for the animal kingdom, or even the planet come to that. Times are changing though and lots of growers are adopting more nature-friendly pest prevention methods that don't involve chemical pesticides. Some of these methods can be easily replicated at home and, trust me, you're going to need them.

My favourite 'friendly' method for protecting plants involves sacrificing some beer. Yep, it's not just humans that love a beverage, slugs and snails are partial to a late-night tipple too, but guess what, they aren't interested in the alcohol. Slugs and snails are completely addicted to yeast and will happily drown themselves in the stuff. Carefully place a plastic tub or cup which is filled two-thirds full with beer and position it near those pristine cabbages to tempt and trap those pesky slugs and snails. I know it's tempting, but try not to use slug pellets – they are pretty devastating when it comes to wildlife and do more harm than good in your garden. You can get some organic slug pellets that contain naturally occurring iron, but this stuff is still poisonous to birds and mammals if they eat a dead slug or snail that has come into contact with slug pellets.

Net everything! Insect netting can solve a lot of your pest woes. Huge nets are used on farms to protect crops and using them at home is really simple and cheap. You can get various mesh sizes that help stop rabbits, birds, butterflies and many other insects accessing your plants. You can simply drape the nets directly on the plants or create a frame/hoop to suspend it above. Try making hoops from wire or old plastic pipes. Remember though, not all insects are bad and you should try to invite them into your growing space if possible. Lots of flowers will attract vegetable-friendly insects that actually like to hunt down the cabbage-munching creepy crawlies.

Rodents are a common issue when growing fruits and veggies, as they love to munch their way through all sorts of seeds, shoots and fully-grown fruit and veg. You can use various traps including 'live catch' systems, but I try to work around the issue by sticking to some simple rules. If you can, sow indoors to keep your seeds and seedlings safe from rodents before planting them outside once they're a little more mature. Use nets or fleece to protect your plants as this can stop even the most ravenous radish-loving rodent. And, if all else fails maybe get a really angry cat. I did!

Finally, keep it clean. Try to remove dead leaves and plants throughout the season as this will help keep disease at bay and you'll disrupt any places where pests might hide. Wash used pots and containers over winter with soapy water to make sure they're pest-free for the next growing season. Also, allow your plants to experience a bit of a breeze, especially if they spend most of their time indoors or in a greenhouse, as a bit of wind helps to reduce bacteria build-up.

ROOTS

Swede

Celeriac

Oca

Garlic

Onions

Sweet potatoes

Ginger

Parsnips

Carrots

Beetroot

Radishes

Potatoes

SWEDE (RUTABAGA)

Yep, you heard right. It's not just called a swede – it has some other funky names too like neep, Swedish turnip and snagger. True to its name, these weird two-tone roots first appeared in Sweden around the fifteenth century and, although it's not a great looker (and commonly fed to farm animals), it is now used in dishes around the world. In the UK, before pumpkins were readily available for Hallowe'en, the rutabaga was carved, lit up and placed in windows to ward off evil spirts. Think I'll stick to carving pumpkins and mashing my swedes. Now, let's get those neeps growing!

What you'll need:
- 1 x 5 L (1.3 US gal) container per two seeds (or a larger container or bed for more)
- Multipurpose compost
- Swede seeds

SOW

Get your swede on in late spring when all signs of frost have past. Fill your container to an inch from the top with compost, ensuring it is squashed down and firm. Using a pencil, make a 2cm (¾in) deep hole in the centre of the container. If sowing multiple seeds in a larger container, space the holes 25cm (10in) apart. Place two seeds in each hole (one acts as a backup) and cover with compost. Give the compost a trickle of water and pop the containers in a sunny spot outside or on a window ledge.

GROW

Keep the soil watered, but not soaked, and after a couple of weeks your neep seedlings will be about 2.5cm (1in) tall. At this stage, you need to remove and discard any extra seedlings so that you've only got one plant per spacing. Allow them to continue growing in their sunny spot while keeping them well watered. Don't let them dry out – the soil should be just damp to the touch.

GATHER

After six months of growth they should be ready to harvest. Move some soil from around the top of the plant using your fingers. If the top of the swede looks nice and bulbous, give it a good tug and out it should come. If you like what you see, then they're ready, although you can eat them at any size. If they're still a little too small for your liking, let them grow for a bit longer (although the tester swede you've pulled up will have to be eaten as it can't be put back). Once they're ready, trim them, wash them off, cook them and mash them up!

TIPS

Being a brassica (it's the family name not a musical instrument), butterflies will be after your swede plants. Never fear, as a small amount of fine netting will protect your plants from these pretty pests and keep them healthy.

I grew up in Cornwall and there's this historic thing called a Cornish pasty. It's a pretty big deal. Anyway, it's got swede in it and if you don't use swede or even think about putting a carrot in it, then people will hurl abuse and banish you from the shire!

CELERIAC

Celery root, turnip rooted-celery and, my personal favourite, knob celery are just a few of the names you'll find for celeriac. This root vegetable has been loitering around for centuries and produces the most creamy, smooth, unusual-tasting mash known to mankind. It's a pretty tough plant with no real pest issues (that I've encountered anyway) and it originates from the Mediterranean. This root vegetable can be eaten at any stage of growth and will store for several months if kept cold enough. Give it a try – why have normal celery when you can have knobbly celery?

What you'll need:
- Seed module trays
- Multipurpose compost
- Celeriac seeds (I like Brilliant and Prinz)
- A final container or bed that's 10L (2.6 US gal) or bigger

SOW

In early spring, fill all the modules in your seed tray with compost, then tap it on a surface to make sure the compost is compacted. Using a pencil, make a small hole, less then 5mm (¼in) deep, in the centre of each cell. Pop one seed in each cell and cover with compost. Give them a gentle water (don't let them dry out), place them on a warm windowsill and allow to germinate (about 7–10 days, but possibly longer as they can be rather erratic).

GROW

Once your plants are 8–10cm (3–4in) high, it's time to plant them out. You'll need a 10L (2.3 US gal) pot for every seedling, or space them 20cm (8in) apart if using a larger container. Fill your container with compost, use your finger to create a small hole that will fit your seedling, then pop it in. Gently push the compost around the seedling to secure it, place in full sun and keep watered.

GATHER

We've arrived in early autumn and, although it's only pumpkins that might be on your mind, it's time to start harvesting those celeriac. Pull a plant out of its container and there should be a large knobbly, grapefruit-sized ball. They are edible at any size, so if it looks a good size to you, then it's time to clean off the mud and get cooking.

TIPS

When you dig up your first celeriac you may be slightly confused as it probably won't be a perfectly round shape, like you find in grocery stores. Instead it will look like a large collection of roots resembling worms (this is how they're meant to look). Hold on to your pants again because, yes, you guessed it – they're edible. Wash them and cut them off, fry and season for some crazy-looking, crispy and creamy celeriac worms!

Watch out for slugs and snails when you first plant out. Try making a beer trap (see page 25).

OCA

Say what? Never heard of it? I'm not surprised, but they are fast becoming one of the most popular root veggies to grow at home. These strange grub-looking Andean tubers come in really vivid colours and have a potato-like taste with a citrus tang. Grown for centuries in the Andes as a staple food source, it is thought that hundreds of different varieties exist, although the diversity is slowly decreasing. They are really easy to grow in containers, providing you don't pack them in like a crowded bus, and they only produce a few hundred grams (a few ounces) of tubers per plant. The whole plant is edible with the stems being sour – perfect as a rhubarb substitute. The plants only produce the tubers during shorter days as winter approaches, so if you're in this for the long haul, then let's get started.

What you'll need:

- Oca tubers (have a play with varieties – I have no favourites, as they all look awesome)
- 1 x 5L (1.3 US gal) container per tuber (or a larger container or bed for more)
- Multipurpose compost

SOW

In early spring, you should put your tubers somewhere light (but not in direct sunlight) and allow them to 'chit' (grow shoots). Once the shoots are 2.5cm (1in) long, it's time to get these funky tubers in some compost.

Fill your container with compost so that it's nearly full. Using your finger, make a hole in the compost around 5–8cm (2–3in) deep (if sowing multiple tubers in a larger container, space the holes 15cm/6in apart). Place your tuber in the hole, with the shoots pointing upwards, and gently cover with a little more compost, ensuring you don't break the shoots. If the leaves haven't formed yet, then you can cover up the shoots; if the leaves have started to form, then make sure they sit above the compost. Give them a light watering and then put them in a sunny spot indoors or outside.

GROW

As the historic saying goes… 'treat them mean, keep them keen'. You don't need to give your oca plants any food and it's best to keep them a little dry as well, so only water them every other day. They are used to harsh conditions and will thrive from a bit of abuse. They have leaves like clover that open in the day and close at night to protect themselves. The more sunlight the better, so don't go hiding them away in a shady corner.

GATHER

In late autumn/early winter, once the foliage of the plant has died back and before the first frost, it's time to empty your container and search for the rainbow-coloured tubers. There should be lots of nuggets of oca waiting for you – wash them off and treat like potatoes.

TIPS

You can grow your tubers in small pots first and keep them indoors to give them a head start before planting them out into their final position or a larger container.

Once harvested, treat those tubers to a nice suntan by popping them on a windowsill for a few days before you intend to cook with them – this will make them much sweeter.

GARLIC

Garlic is a great way of stopping your partner from kissing you, it's perfect at keeping vampires away, and it's also a really simple plant to grow at home. Native to Central Asia and used for thousands of years in cookery and medicine, it's no surprise that China produces over 21 million tons of the stuff each year. Garlic comes in 'softneck' and 'hardneck' varieties. Softnecks are best suited to warmer climates and store for much longer, whereas hardnecks are much hardier in colder climates and have a better flavour. There are hundreds of different varieties of garlic, but most of them are hardneck and each is suited to a different region and country. Choose what you think is best for you, but I've suggested a couple of my favourite varieties to the right.

What you'll need:
- 1 x 5L (1.3 US gal) container per set (clove) (or a larger container or bed for more – these are perfect for raised beds)
- Multipurpose compost
- Garlic sets (Red Duke and Iberian Wight are great)

SOW

Garlic should be planted in late autumn/early winter as they need a cold spell to help kick them into gear. Fill your chosen container or bed with compost, 2.5cm (1in) from the top. Push each individual set (pointed bit facing up) just below the surface. Sow each set in the centre of a 5L (1.3 US gal) pot, or sow them 10cm (4in) apart if sowing in a bed or larger container. Give them a water and place them outside in a sunny spot. That's it!

GROW

Make sure they don't dry out too much, so water occasionally, avoiding them sitting in soaking wet soil as this will cause them to rot.

GATHER

You can begin to harvest in late spring/early summer when the garlic leaves have turned yellow and are dying off. Lift the bulbs with a small fork or spade, brush the soil off and let them dry on a rack or table in a sunny spot for 1–2 weeks. If you want to be a proper show-off you can try plaiting them together, but this will only work with softneck varieties.

Once dry, your garlic is ready to use. Sit back and give those vampires something to think about!

TIPS

There's an elephant in the room! I mean elephant garlic. You can't miss it (it's massive). This variety had been lost until 1941 when it was discovered growing wild in the USA. It has a milder flavour compared to standard garlic and is definitely worth trying to grow if you want to impress your friends. Just follow the steps above using elephant garlic sets.

You can further satisfy your garlicky fetish by eating garlic 'scapes', which are the flower buds that appear on hardneck varieties of garlic. These can be cooked and made into yummy things like pesto and hummus, or roasted like a garlicky asparagus-style treat.

ONIONS

Onions can bring people to tears in the kitchen, but they're one of the most widely grown and used vegetables in the world. Just to blow your onion-growing mind, as a planet we produce over 93 million tons of onions each year – just think of the smell! Being one of the world's oldest cultivated vegetables and thought to come from Asia, it's no surprise they have been used medicinally in the past and were popular in days gone by due to their long storage life when dried. You can grow onions from seed, but us gardeners love a shortcut, so I recommend buying some immature bulbs called 'onion sets' to get yourself started. There are plenty of varieties to choose from and you can use this method for shallots too.

What you'll need:

- 1 x 5L (1.3 US gal) container per set (or a larger container or bed for more – these are perfect for raised beds)
- Multipurpose compost
- Onion sets (Centurion and Red Baron work well)

SOW

You can sow sets from mid- to late spring. Fill your chosen pots, container or bed with compost to 2.5cm (1in) from the top. Crack open your sets and you'll see they have a pointed top and a round bottom with small roots. Push each set into the compost, pointed top facing up and so it's no more than two-thirds buried. Sow each set in the centre of a 5L (1.3 US gal) pot, or sow them at least 10cm (4in) apart if sowing in a bed or larger container (remember they will grow into a full-sized onion). Place them outside in a sunny spot and give them a gentle watering.

GROW

Keep them watered and watch the magic happen as they sprout and grow over the next few months. Make sure they don't dry out too much, but equally you don't want them sitting in soaking wet soil as this will cause them to rot.

GATHER

It's late summer, you've got a great tan and eaten lots of veg, but you're desperate to try the onions. Well, as soon as the tops turn yellow and the leaves flop over you can pick your homegrown tear-inducing bulbs. Place the onions off the ground on a rack or table in full sun to dry for at least 8–10 days. Keep cool if you're storing them, otherwise get cooking and let the tears commence.

TIPS

If you really love onions, then you're in luck because sets can be sown in autumn as well as in spring, ensuring year-round feasting.

SWEET POTATOES

Often incorrectly called yams, but correctly called kumara, batatas and uala in New Zealand, South America and Hawaii, sweet potatoes are, in fact, not potatoes at all. They're not my favourite root vegetable to eat, but I do enjoy growing them and there are several unusual types, like a purple-fleshed variety, that are really fun to grow.

Having lived in New Zealand for a while and consumed my body weight in avocados and sweet potatoes, I soon realized how inexpensive sweet potatoes were compared to countries where they are not commercially produced. Originating from South America, the way you grow these starchy tubers is to use 'slips', which are the shoots you get when a tuber sprouts. You can create these slips yourself, but it's much easier to buy them like you would seeds. With a bit of sunshine and love you'll impress all your friends with homegrown sweet potato fries (or whatever else you come up with).

What you'll need:

- Sweet potato slips (Carolina Ruby and Molokai are my favourites)
- A large container or raised bed at least 60 x 60cm (2 x 2ft) wide and 30m (1ft) deep
- Multipurpose compost
- Plastic bag/sheet to cover the soil

SOW

Put your slips in a glass of water so that the stem is submerged as soon as they arrive in late spring. Wait for about a week until they start to grow roots (you can skip this bit if your slips arrived in soil). Once you've got some roots, fill your chosen container almost to the top with compost and use your plastic bag/sheet to cover the soil, tucking it in around the edges. This plastic will help heat up the soil and keep it warm. Now, cut a small cross through the plastic at each location you want to plant a slip. Carefully push the slips through the plastic and into the compost, with the roots facing downwards. I'd put no more than two slips in a 60cm (2ft) square container. Carefully water each plant and keep the container indoors or in a warm, sheltered spot outside.

GROW

Sweet potatoes like it hot, and the plastic will heat up the soil so it's nice and toasty. If you want to help your plants out, then you can put them in a greenhouse or create a mini plastic tunnel over the container to trap even more heat.

Keep the plants well watered but not soaked. Sweet potatoes have lovely flowers, so make sure to show them to everyone that visits while they're growing.

GATHER

You can gently dig up your tubers after around five months of growth, or once the foliage turns yellow. Congratulations, you're now the proud owner of some sweet potatoes.

TIPS

These plants really do love heat. If you're happy to have a rambling sweet potato plant in your house and you've got a room with plenty of natural light, then that's the way to go – these roots were made for people who lack garden space or even a garden at all.

Also, apparently sweet potato cheesecake is rather tasty, but don't take my word for it.

GINGER

Well blow my beard off! If you didn't know already, ginger has some great things going for it. It has amazing medicinal and culinary uses in both sweet and savoury dishes, but it can also bring people to tears with its fiery nature. It originates from Taiwan and was sold across Asia back in the day, where it became the first exported spice. We clearly can't get enough of the stuff, as over 2.8 million tons is grown and harvested each year. Growing ginger is so simple, you really have to give it a go.

What you'll need:

- A fairly shallow container of any size, that you can easily keep indoors (minimum 1L/1 US qt container per piece of ginger)
- A 50/50 mix of multipurpose compost and seed compost
- The freshest looking bit of root ginger you can find from a grocery store
- Clear plastic bag, large enough to fit over your container

SOW

Personally, I think early spring is the best time to sow ginger, but you really can do it any time of the year. Fill your container 90 per cent full with your compost mix. Find the 'eye' on the end of your bit of root ginger (this is where it will sprout from) and cut off a big toe-sized piece. Bury as many of these pieces as you can fit in the container, with the 'eye' facing upwards just below the surface, but don't overcrowd it. Dust over a little more compost so that they're just covered. Give it a splash of water, put a plastic bag over the top and place it somewhere warm indoors – a windowsill is perfect. Wasn't that simple?

GROW

Keep them moist. Once you see your ginger beginning to shoot you can remove the bag that's been covering them. You'll have to keep your plants indoors in a bright spot, especially in winter, but in the summer they can go in a greenhouse or cold frame if you prefer.

GATHER

Although ginger is very simple to grow, it does take quite a long time. After eight months of growth, the tops of the plants should die back and you can start to harvest some ginger. Have a rummage, pull those roots out the pot and your ginger should emerge.

TIPS

If you like what you see and taste, then why not replant some pieces of ginger you've just gathered and start the process over again?

PARSNIPS

Every year my mother sends me an inappropriately titled message containing a photo of my father's giant parsnips… You can be disgusted by this white root veg all you want, but they can be pretty impressive. I understand that the sweet taste is an acquired one, but with the likes of celebrity chefs transforming them into soups, mousses, purées, crisps and that weird foam stuff, it's only a matter of time before you're converted into a parsnip lover. Growing and pulling your own huge parsnip out the ground, you'll not only impress yourself, but also anyone you go thrusting it at. Parsnips are native to Eurasia and although in ancient historical writings they are difficult to distinguish from carrots, they were quite popular. In Europe, the parsnip was used as a source of sugar before beet and cane sugars were readily available. Could I get a lump of parsnip in my coffee please?

What you'll need:

- Any type of container as long as it's got good drainage and is 40cm (16in) or deeper
- Multipurpose compost
- Parsnip seeds (Gladiator and Albion are great)
- Insect mesh
- Gardening gloves

SOW

You want to sow parsnips in late spring (if you sow any earlier your plants will struggle). Fill the container you've chosen until it's 5cm (2in) from the top and then place your seeds on the surface (two seeds per 2.5cm/1in square). Cover with 3.5cm (1½in) of compost, water gently and place somewhere light and warm. Your journey to parsnip enlightenment has begun!

GROW

Parsnips are not Olympic sprinters when it comes to germinating, so you will have to be patient. Keep them damp and they should germinate after 7–12 days. Once they've germinated and are big enough to handle (about 2.5cm/1in tall) you need to pinch out carefully and discard all but one seedling every 8cm (3in), so that the parsnips left in the soil have space to mature and grow into hefty roots (this is called 'thinning out'). Move them outside and keep them watered but not drenched.

Parsnips are related to carrots and that means if you've got carrot flies around, they will go after the parsnips as well. To stop them, just keep the top of your container 60cm (2ft) aboe ground level or wrap it with insect mesh. You're done, give yourself a high five and leave them to grow.

GATHER

Early autumn is time to give your parsnips a tug, or once you start to see the foliage die back. If you leave your plants in the ground to experience a couple of frosts it will make them even sweeter. Wearing gloves, you can pull the plants up out of the soil as and when you need them.

TIPS

Burn baby burn! Try not to touch the foliage – I'm serious, as the sap can give you a burn called *phytophotodermatitis*. The sap reacts with sunlight on your skin, so harvesting them on a cloudy day will help reduce the risk, but please also make sure you wear gloves.

CARROTS

Now, I know what you're thinking: carrots are these boring orange things that never actually help you to see in the dark and they can't really be grown in a small space. Well, hold onto your night vision goggles as I'm about to blow your carrot-growing mind. Carrots never used to be just orange – the orange colour is likely due to a Dutch cultivation that happened in the sixteenth and seventeenth centuries, which became very popular. Luckily, we haven't lost the original carrot colours and you can now grow some super-psychedelic carrots including yellow, white, purple and red varieties. There are also some fun little round orange varieties that taste great and don't need lots of deep soil to grow in.

What you'll need:

- Any type of deep container or a small raised bed. Buckets work really well, but shallow trays are also great for round varieties as they don't need much depth
- 50/50 mix of multipurpose compost and horticultural sand
- Carrot seeds (my favourites are Globe, Paris Market, Rainbow Mix and Purple Haze)
- Insect mesh

SOW

You can sow your carrot seeds anytime from early spring till late summer. Fill your container almost to the top with your compost and sand mix. Sow the carrot seeds in rows or scatter them thinly (I find this works best) over the compost mix and then add another thin layer – no more than 1cm (less than ½in) – of compost mix on top. Give them a gentle drink of water and then pop them somewhere light, indoors or outside, and you should see some action in 7–10 days.

GROW

Make sure your carrot seedlings are kept watered but not soaked.

In the world of carrots there is only one main enemy – the carrot root fly. Luckily, they can only fly up to 60cm (2ft), so if your garden is on a balcony or your containers are more than 60cm (2ft) tall, then there's no need to worry. However, if your plants are at risk from carrot root fly, then you'll need to protect them with an insect mesh barrier wrapped around the top of your chosen container or bed.

Four to five weeks after sowing, you need to thin out the carrot seedlings. Carefully pinch out and discard all but one seedling every 2–3cm (1in) so that the carrots left in the soil have space to mature.

GATHER

It takes 60–80 days for a carrot crop to mature. Have a little rummage around the top of each plant to check for a decent girth on your carrot top. If you like what you feel, carefully give them a tug and pull them out of the soil, wash them and then feel free to try out your best Bugs Bunny impression.

TIPS

If you sow a new packet of seeds every two weeks you should end up with a great carrot supply throughout the growing season.

Touching the foliage attracts carrot flies so it really helps if you leave them alone.

Avoid feeding your carrots with anything overly nutritious as this will cause multiple roots and your carrots will look like an octopus!

BEETROOT

Check out my sick beets! Beetroot, sea beet, Harvard beets or blood turnip. Whatever you call them there's more to beetroot than staining your fingers, ruining every chopping board in your house or turning your urine pink. What I love most about them is that they come in lots of different colours – yellow, white, pink and a beautiful stripey variety called Chioggia, all of which should make you stand up and consider growing them at home. Beetroot has been eaten throughout history for nutrition and medicinal purposes.

What you'll need:

- Large pot, trough or container (2L/2 US qt minimum per plant)
- Multipurpose compost or fertile soil
- Beetroot seeds (Chioggia is a must, as well as Golden)

SOW

Growing massive beetroots is a waste of nutrients, especially in a small space, and gives you a poor-flavoured crop. So, (for once in my life) I'm advocating small balls rather than big ones. It's best to sow your beet seeds thinly in rows from mid-spring until midsummer. Fill your chosen container with compost so its nearly full. Using a pencil, make 1cm (½in) deep holes in rows spaced 12–14cm (about 5in) apart, leaving a 20cm (8in) gap between each row. Place a seed in each hole and then cover them over with a little more compost. Give them a drink of water and pop them somewhere warm and light – near a window is great. Later in the season you can sow them directly outside if you're using a large, raised bed or container.

GROW

Once they have germinated and are a couple of weeks old you can move them outside. Keep them in their current container or replant straight into the ground. Make sure they are well watered and watch them grow.

GATHER

After two months, your beetroots should be ready to harvest. If you haven't already gone in hands-first and had a rummage, then now's the time. Carefully tug those colourful balls out of the ground and give them a wash. Beetroots have a high sugar content, so feel free to eat them raw, pickle them, boil them or make them into one of those weird health smoothies. Just enjoy them, you beetroot-growing master!

TIPS

All parts of the beetroot plant are edible (and really tasty). The stems and leaves are also delicious – chuck them into salads or use them like you would Swiss chard.

RADISHES

I was once told that radishes have nothing to offer apart from their watery taste that lures you in and then smacks you round the chops with a fiery bitter afterburn. Personally, I couldn't be happier with that and since discovering the beautiful patterns that Asian varieties have to offer, and some great-tasting varieties such as French Breakfast, I'm happy to have a few growing in my garden all year round. Radishes were probably domesticated in both Europe and Asia separately and the name radish comes from the Latin word *radix* which, funnily enough, means root! All parts of the plant can be eaten and some are grown just for the seeds, which are turned into oil.

What you'll need:

- Anything that holds soil – pots, trays or even a cut open milk carton!
- Multipurpose compost
- Radish seeds (I love French Breakfast, Blue Moon, Watermelon and Rainbow Mixed)

SOW

Radishes can be sown from early spring until late summer, but the Asian varieties prefer it to be cooler and should be sown from late summer onwards, otherwise they will bolt (flower) and leave you with no root to eat.

Fill your chosen container with compost; don't go too crazy and overfill it, three-quarters full will be fine. The seeds are small but fairly easy to handle – I like to place them a fingers-width apart in rows, or randomly scattered, across the surface of the soil. Cover with a thin layer of compost, gently water and… you're done. If your house is particularly cold, then you could try growing them inside, but it's best to place them outside so they don't get too hot (sunshine isn't an issue for these guys, just the actual warmth of the air temperature around them).

GROW

Don't forget about the radishes! They will germinate and grow really fast, so they need lots of water. Also try to keep them off the ground as slugs and snails love a late-night radish snack. They should be ready to eat four weeks from sowing. Pretty simple hey?

GATHER

Radishes aren't shy and you'll be able to see when they are ready as their colourful tops will be bulging out of the soil. Pull up one to have a look and just pick them when you're happy with the size. Leaving them to become too big will make them super-peppery and a bit woody.

TIPS

Sowing radish seeds every couple of weeks will give you an ongoing supply as they have such a fast growth rate.

I like to roast my radishes whole. Fun fact: you can also eat the radish seed pods for a crisp, spicy burst.

Leaving a few plants unharvested to flower will make your growing space look even more gorgeous, and will also attract butterflies away from your brassicas.

POTATOES

Potatoes, spuds, taters, *pommes de terre*. Whatever you call them, it's clear that the world can't get enough of them. Having originated from South America, there are now more than 4,000 varieties of potato available worldwide. We've become used to eating the classic white potato, but what if I told you that you can grow some absolutely crazy-coloured, great-tasting potatoes in a container at home? I'm talking purple, red, pink, as well as lots of beautiful patterns. Let's get growing...

What you'll need:

- A 30L (8 US gal) container (or use an old bin or sack – anything that has good depth and will retain water)
- Multipurpose compost
- Seed potatoes (I like Red Emmalie, Salad Blue and Edzell)

SOW

In early to mid-spring (depending on the potato variety), fill up one-third of your container with compost, chuck two to three potatoes in, then fill the other third. Give the compost a good drink of water and place in a sunny spot; this can be indoors under a window or outside – just make sure that there's plenty of light and keep that compost damp. That's it. It's really that easy.

GROW

OK, you've waited two to three weeks – hopefully you haven't killed them (don't forget to water) and by now you should have a lovely bit of bushy greenery peeping out of the top of the compost. Now, I know it sounds a bit crazy, but I want you to bury all that fresh growth with more compost. What this does is encourage a second tier of potatoes to grow underneath the soil, so you can gather as many as possible come harvesting time.

Leave them to grow again and become a small forest, while continuing to keep the soil damp. Flowers will start to appear and we need to remove them as this will help increase the size of your new potatoes that are forming. Pick off the flowers and dispose of them – do NOT save or eat the flowers as they are poisonous!

GATHER

Finally, the time has come to stuff your face with starchy goodness. Once your potato forest starts to die back a little, wait patiently for another two weeks. Then it's time to harvest. Remove the stems and discard them. Now, scoop out as much compost as you can from the container and start rummaging around for potatoes with your hands. Sometimes, I find it useful to tip out the contents of the container to make sure I don't miss any. Give them a good sniff (earthy and delicious), scrub them in the sink, then prep for eating. There's nothing quite like eating purple mash or red fries...

TIPS

Chit this out! If you'd like to give your seed potatoes a kick up the behind and encourage them to grow faster once planted, then why not chit them before planting? Place them in a warm, dark spot (a cupboard will do) and leave them alone until they grow lots of small shoots. Then follow the above instructions.

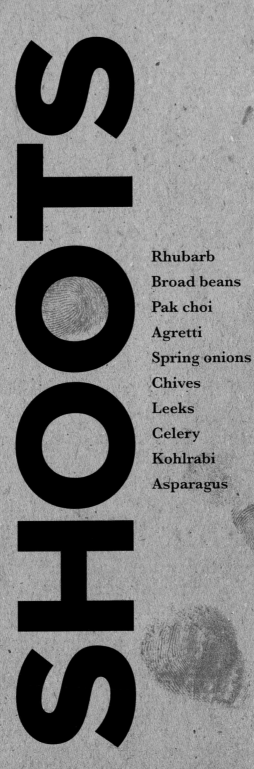

SHOOTS

Rhubarb

Broad beans

Pak choi

Agretti

Spring onions

Chives

Leeks

Celery

Kohlrabi

Asparagus

RHUBARB

You can thank me later, because growing rhubarb is SO easy, I almost don't know why I'm bothering to tell you. Firstly, there's no messing about with seeds – you pretty much always use either crowns, which are young established plants, or pieces, which are cut off older plants. Secondly, they need little care, can be really portable in the right container and will produce loads of stems for at least 10 years! Rhubarb comes from Asia and has been cultivated for at least 3,000 years, if not longer. For centuries, it was used medicinally (the roots are a laxative, remember that for later) and it's only in the past 200 or so years that it has been used as a culinary ingredient. If you don't grow any at home, you're a fool, a rhubarb fool!

What you'll need:

- A 40L (10.5 US gal) container or bigger will give you a decent crop
- Manure
- Soil-based compost (John Innes or similar)
- Rhubarb crowns or pieces (I like Fultons Strawberry Surprise and Champagne)

SOW

You can buy and plant your rhubarb in either autumn or spring, as long as it's not too cold. Put a decent layer of manure in the bottom of your container and fill up with compost. Using your hands or a trowel, make a hole in the centre that's big enough for the rhubarb crown/piece. You want to bury the rhubarb just above the soil level so a bud is showing. If water sits on the surface the bud will rot, so we want to avoid this. Place outside and water carefully. Mission complete.

GROW

Leave your plant alone and let it do its thing. Unless you were given a huge established plant, you shouldn't pick anything off it yet. Let your rhubarb grow in the first year after planting and keep it well watered.

GATHER

After a year, you can pick stems from mid-spring to early summer each year. Always try to leave 2–3 stems on the plant at any one time so it doesn't struggle. Don't cut the stems off as this can cause rot; instead, gently pull the stem from side to side until it comes loose at the base. As long as you keep picking, it should keep growing. Time for a crumble, I think.

Oh and one last thing… please don't eat the leaves, they're poisonous.

TIPS

If you want bright pink rhubarb, then why not 'force' it? This essentially means that you block out all sunlight from the plant using a cloche or bucket, thereby 'forcing' it to grow fast and early so that it produces blood red stems. Apply manure or feed every autumn to help them in the following spring and split the plant every six years to keep it productive.

BROAD BEANS

Also known as fava or faba beans and originating from the eastern Mediterranean, these legumes are an old plant – probably one of the first crops used in ancient agriculture. They're hardy and easy to grow.

Broad beans are a really versatile plant that can be sown in autumn, but more commonly in early spring. You can eat not only the beans (broad bean pâté is a must) but also the pods and the tops of the plants. Most varieties are similar, with only the flowering time and pod size changing, but there are a few red bean varieties that are worth a try. I think every growing space should have these beans in, not only for your belly but for the huge number of bees and insects that they will attract.

What you'll need:
- Broad bean seeds (give Karmazyn or De Monica a try)
- A tub or pot (at least 10L/2.6 US gal) – an old sink works well
- Multipurpose compost

SOW

If you bought a hardy variety, it will say if you can sow it in autumn or just spring. The night before you start your bean adventure, soak your bean seeds overnight in a small amount of water. This helps them to germinate and not rot. Fill your container almost to the top with compost. With a finger, poke 5cm (2in) deep holes spaced 20cm (8in) apart. If you're using a smaller pot (about 5L/1.3 US gal) I'd sow no more than two seeds per pot. Place your seeds in the holes, cover them over with a thin layer of compost, then gently water and place indoors or outside in a warm sunny spot.

GROW

After seven days, the beans should germinate. These will continue to grow inside, but move them outside if you can. You'll want to give the plants a hand by adding some support in the form of canes or string (see page 22). This will give them something to climb up and also protect them from strong winds that might knock them over. Keep watered.

GATHER

If you sowed your beans in autumn, then by mid- to late spring you should have some decent plants. If you did an early spring sowing, then wait until the plants look big enough – about 90–120cm (3–4ft) tall. The plants should have already flowered lower down and pods will be forming; wait until the pods are a good size and then you can pick and harvest the beans inside. My preferred parts of the plant are the shoots at the top. Pinch out a decent number of tops (the growing tip) off each plant. Doing this will also help prevent black fly. Give the tops a wash and boil them up. Tasty, right? Now, go forth and tell everyone about the wondrous broad bean tops.

TIPS

If you're growing in small pots and want some decent beans, then a liquid feed every two to three weeks will help.

Have you tried eating broad bean pods? Shell the beans from the pods, cut up the pods into bite-size pieces, dip them in tempura batter and fry for some super-tasty bean-flavoured chips.

PAK CHOI

Yes, you can successfully grow Asian vegetables at home. This stuff is just brilliant to grow and works well if you can keep the slugs at bay. Also known as Chinese cabbage, bok choi or pok choi, this leafy green brassica originates from China and looks just as good in the garden as it does on your plate. Growing pak choi in a raised bed, basket or container works well and will help keep them healthy and free from damage. If you search for seeds, you'll soon discover several smaller varieties, as well as green and purple. Oh, and finally, don't eat too much as it can be toxic in large quantities!

What you'll need:

- A container, basket or window box, 2L (2 US qt) minimum (a basket is great if you want to avoid slugs)
- Multipurpose compost
- Pak choi seeds (try Joi Choi or Purple)

SOW

Sow the seeds in mid- to late spring. Fill the container with compost almost to the top. Draw a 2cm (¾in) deep line in the soil with your finger and pop the seeds in the row, thinly spaced (seed spacing doesn't matter too much at this stage as you'll thin them out later). If you're doing more than one row, you'll want the rows to be about 10cm (4in) apart. Cover the seeds with a little more compost, add a dribble of water and you're done. Outside in a sunny spot is the best place for these plants to thrive.

GROW

Now, you don't want these plants to get carried away and flower, so make sure they are always well watered. Once they are 2.5cm (1in) or so tall, thin them out by carefully pinching out all but one seedling every 12cm (5in), so that the plants left in the soil have space to mature and bush out. Don't throw away the seedlings you've just pinched out – they are already edible at this stage and they're great thrown in a salad or stir-fry.

GATHER

You can be in pak choi heaven after around 30-odd days from sowing, but it really depends on what size you prefer them to be when cooking. Carefully pull them up or cut them off at the base. If they taste great, it's stir-fries all week.

TIPS

If you want to mix things up a bit, rather than sowing in neat lines, you can multi-sow your pak choi. Simply sprinkle the seeds across the compost within the whole area you want to grow in, then keep well watered in a sunny spot. Harvest them when they're only 5–7cm (2–3in) tall and cook them whole.

Always remember there's no need to be ashamed of buying a few vegetable plug plants and growing them on instead of sowing seeds. It's slightly more expensive, but you'll still end up with some great fresh greens.

AGRETTI

Monk's/friar's beard, saltwort, Roscano. Once used in glassmaking, this Mediterranean bush has changed its ways and become a fashionable plant to toss on top of your Michelin-starred main courses. Most people won't have heard of it, but more market gardens are starting to grow it. Why Sam? Well, firstly it's a great substitute for wild samphire, which is an expensive thing to forage for. Before you say, 'Sam, it's easy to find samphire by the sea, I went foraging, found some straight away and filled my leather satchel.' Well, the key there is you have to be near the sea and that's a luxury not available to everyone. What's more, agretti grows fast and crazy (like my beard), which is handy when you want to use it all the time. Cooked, it's a little like spinach; raw, it's salty with a nice crisp crunch. Roll up your sleeves and give these verdant fronds a try, you won't regret it.

What you'll need:

- Seed module tray
- Multipurpose compost
- Agretti seeds (the fresher the better)
- Raised bed or large container (5 L / 1.3 US gal minimum)

SOW

You can sow indoors from early spring. Fill the seed tray three-quarters full with compost and use a pencil or your finger to poke 1cm (½in) deep holes spaced 8cm (3in) apart. Put one seed in each hole and then cover with a thin layer of compost. Place them somewhere warm indoors and keep them watered. Germination can be a bit hit and miss, but some seedlings should appear after seven days.

GROW

Pot on! When the agretti plants are 8cm (3in) high pot them on into the bigger container. Fill the container up to the top with compost, make small holes 20cm (8in) apart with your fingers, then pop a seedling into each. Press gently around each plant to secure it in place, then lightly water. You can place this container inside near a window or outside and it should be happy. Keep it watered!

GATHER

Once a large bush has formed around early summer, you can start to pick the agretti as and when you need it. It's one of those plants that grows the more you pick it – you'll be fed up with it in no time at all!

TIPS

Don't let the plants get too dry as they can become quite woody and, subsequently, inedible. Seeds can be sown directly into a larger container outside (rather than sowing into a seed tray as I've outlined above) but you want to wait until the temperatures are slightly warmer in mid- to late spring.

SPRING ONIONS

Oh, for the love of God, not more alliums! If things weren't getting smelly enough in this book, I've decided to add another friendly onion. These mild-tasting onion relatives are great for sowing directly outside and need little care. Spring onions originate from Asia and have been used in cooking for centuries. You can get white and red varieties, both of which taste great and can be eaten raw or cooked. I tend to pick them before they get any junk in their trunk and produce a hefty bulb downstairs. They can be grown just after the last frost, hence the name *spring* onion.

What you'll need:

- A pot, raised bed, or hanging basket (5L/ 1.3 US gal minimum)
- Multipurpose compost
- Spring onion seeds (I like Feast or Apache)

SOW

After the first frost, fill your tub nearly to the top with compost. You can then either sow the seeds in neat rows 1cm (½in) deep, or scatter them evenly over the surface and then cover with another 1cm (½in) of compost. I don't mind which method you choose, honest. If they're not outside already, move them to a sunny spot and water carefully. That was easy.

GROW

Don't let them dry out too much. If things are looking a little bushy, then remove a few to give the others space. They're pretty low-maintenance!

GATHER

After all this easy growing you can now pick your spring onions. Some people will tell you the exact size to the millimetre by which you should pick them, but I say do it when you want. If you like them small, pick them when they're small (around two months of growth). If you like them massive, pick them when they're massive (around four months of growth).

TIPS

If you've enjoyed this experience and want more, then why not try sowing a few seeds every couple of weeks? That way you can have fresh spring onion breath all summer.

Give the red-skinned varieties a whirl – I think they're a looker compared to the common white version.

CHIVES

Please stop buying little plastic packets of herbs, especially when it's so simple to grow them at home. Chives have been cultivated by man for thousands of years and are native to a lot of places around the world, mainly North America, Europe and Asia. There are so many different recipes that need that little chive hit and when you've got fresh chives growing at home, you'll use them even more. Not only do they taste really good, they can also repel unwanted garden pests with their pungent aroma.

What you'll need:

- Small pot/container (4L/1 US gal per plant) or bed/tub for multiple plants
- Multipurpose compost
- Chive seeds (I'm not too fussed which ones, they are all similar)

SOW

In early spring, fill a pot with compost to 2.5cm (1in) from the top. Sprinkle a few seeds across the surface and cover with a fine layer of compost, not too much. Give them a careful watering and pop on a windowsill. Give yourself a pat on the back.

GROW

Once your chives have started to fill the pot you can split them and replant in more pots or in a bed so they have space to grow. Make sure you harden them off over a couple of days by leaving them outside during the day, then bringing them in at night – this will wean them off the warmer temperature of your house.

GATHER

Don't go in with your scissors like a wannabe hairdresser. Carefully cut your chives when they look tall enough and only take what you need – too much abuse will make them struggle or even kill them. Chives die back in autumn and will reappear in spring, so don't panic when they disappear; just cut back any dead foliage. Now, throw yourself a chive party and never again purchase herbs in a packet.

TIPS

Personally, I sometimes like to cheat and save time by buying young plants from garden centres or online. Herbs are great for this – you can just pot on the young plants once you get them home.

Chive flowers are a bonus of growing chives – not only do they attract lots of insects, but they are also completely edible. Chuck a few on some lettuce or in a potato salad, however, don't be fooled by their beauty; on an onion-breath-scale these are a ten.

LEEKS

I'm taking a leek and you can't stop me! Native to the Middle East and the Mediterranean, leeks are not the most exciting of vegetables but great to use if you're not the biggest fan of its strong-tasting relatives, like onion and garlic. Having harvested trays of leeks over the years, there's something quite satisfying when trimming them up, peeling back the outer sheath and revealing the bright white flesh beneath.

What you'll need:

- Seed module tray
- Multipurpose compost
- Leek seeds (try Northern Lights or Porbella)
- Container or bed, the bigger and deeper the better

SOW

In early spring, fill up your seed tray with compost and make a 1cm (½in) deep hole in each compartment with your finger. Place one seed in each hole, then cover with a little more compost. Give them a water and place them somewhere warm indoors to grow. Keep the soil damp.

GROW

When your seedlings are around 15cm (6in) long you can fill up your chosen container (an old bath tub would work well) with compost, but don't go overfilling it. Go crazy with your finger or a dibber and make some holes that are 12–13cm (5in) apart, and as deep as the leek seedling stems. If, like me, you like things to be orderly, then arrange them in neat rows, but it doesn't really matter. Pop a leek seedling in each hole but don't surround or cover them with compost. With a bit of watering witchcraft, you can get the surrounding compost to fall into the holes as you soak them. Allowing the compost to wash into the holes gives them a soft cavity into which the plants can expand. Ensure the container sits outside in a sunny spot and don't let the leeks dry out as they grow. Mission complete.

GATHER

When should you take a leek? They will take 24–40 weeks from sowing to mature, but you can eat them at any stage. I prefer mine on the small side as I love to roast them whole. Using a small fork, or simply your hands, gently tug them out of the ground, give them a rinse and voilà.

TIPS

Bury the shaft! Yep, you heard me right. Banking up soil or compost around the leek stems as they grow will help to produce longer and whiter stems.

The world record for the heaviest leek is a ridiculous 10.7kg (23½lb), so if you'd like to grow a whopper, then be sure to nourish your leeks every couple of weeks with a liquid feed.

CELERY

'Sam, I don't like celery because it's stringy and it tastes of water.' Well, guess what, that's your problem, not mine! I love celery and it's not just white and green. You can get some beautiful Asian pink varieties and some great red varieties that can add colour, not only to your growing space, but also to a fairly average salad.

Wild versions have been found across Europe, but it is thought to have originated in the Mediterranean and was domesticated as a vegetable in the seventeenth century with a strong taste and a slightly hollow stem. Fast-forward, and after years of selective breeding, we have the modern celery that's used all over the world. If you're worried it's too healthy, never fear, as I'm sure you can find a calorific dip to accompany the stalks.

What you'll need:

- Seed module tray
- Multipurpose compost
- Celery seeds (try Chinese Pink or Giant Red)
- A 5L (1.3 US gal) tub or pot per plant, or raised bed
- General liquid feed

SOW

In mid-spring, fill up a module tray with compost. Using a pencil or your finger, make a small 1cm (½in) deep hole in the centre of each module. Add one seed per hole, cover over with a little more compost, water carefully and place the tray somewhere inside that's warm and light. Celery likes to be warm, especially when germinating, so try to keep them at 15°C (59°F) or above. Now be patient – they can take up to 20 days to germinate.

GROW

Never ever let your celery dry out. Not only will I shed a tear but your celery will suffer as a huge percentage of a fully grown celery plant is water. When the young plants have filled the modules with their roots, it's almost time to transplant them. Firstly, we need to get them used to being outside, so place the seed trays outside during the day for a week, bringing them inside again each night. Once they're accustomed to cooler temperatures, fill a 5L (1.3 US gal) pot with compost, make a hole in the centre just big enough to fit one celery seedling, then carefully remove one seedling from the module and pop it in the hole. Secure with your fingers and give it a good water. Repeat with the remaining seedlings. Alternatively, plant your celery seedlings 20cm (8in) apart in a larger container or raised bed. Ensure the celery plants are in a sunny spot and water regularly. Feed every two to three weeks with liquid feed in the summer. That's it!

GATHER

It's late summer/early autumn and your celery should be looking magnificent. No tugging is allowed! Get your favourite sharp knife and cut the plant off level with the soil. Give it a wash and it's ready to eat. I've heard it goes well with peanut butter.

TIPS

The process of 'blanching' involves preventing any light getting to the celery stems as they grow. This reduces the bitterness of celery and makes it sweeter, so why not try wrapping the stems with cardboard or covering them with a piece of drainpipe? This will also make the stems as white as a celebrity's teeth. Some varieties planted closer together will self-blanch and turn white without any help.

KOHLRABI

This strange vegetable will really blow your mind and doesn't taste anything like you think it would. Saying that, consuming it raw is like eating a slightly sweet cabbage and nut-flavoured, crisp apple, which does sound really weird but it tastes great, honest. As far as vegetables go, it's pretty odd-looking with its swollen stem and leaves that appear all over it. You can get a purple version and a white one, both taste lovely and you can have summer, autumn and winter crops depending on when you sow them. The word kohl comes from the German for cabbage and rabi is a type of turnip, but it didn't originate in Germany. It appeared in north-east Europe in the sixteenth century and was probably a crazy natural hybrid, but nobody really knows. If you've never tried growing it you should definitely give it a go.

What you'll need:
- Seed module tray
- Multipurpose compost
- Kohlrabi seeds (I love Korfu and Ballot)
- A raised bed or container (5L/1.3 US gal minimum)

SOW

You can sow from mid-spring onwards until late summer. Fill a seed tray with compost and tap it down so it's not too loose. With a pencil or dibber, make a small hole 1cm (½in) deep in the centre of each cell. Pop one seed in each module and cover with compost. Give them a gentle water, pop them on a warm windowsill and allow to germinate. Don't let them dry out.

GROW

Once each seedling has filled the module with its roots and is about 8cm (3in) tall, you can plant it into your chosen container. You need about 18cm (7in) between plants, so squeeze in as many as you think will fit the space. Keep them outside in a sunny spot and don't let the soil dry out. Sit back and relax.

GATHER

Your funky swollen stems should be ready to eat at around 50 days, or when they are 5–7cm (2–3in) wide. Pull them out from the soil and trim the leaves, stems and roots off so you're left with the root ball. Go crazy and invite all your friends round to try it raw as a snack, or grated into coleslaw, but just make sure you peel it first.

TIPS

If you love kohlrabi, then why not sow a few each month to give yourself endless cropping from summer until Christmas?

You might want to keep them netted if you have lots of other brassicas nearby as they will attract butterflies; swiftly followed by caterpillars.

ASPARAGUS

It's time to talk about the only vegetable known to make your urine smell while also acting as an aphrodisiac! Asparagus originates from the Mediterranean, although wild plants have been found in Africa as well. Plants produce 'spears', which are the bit we eat, and can keep producing for up to 25 years.

Before we start, I need to make you aware that growing asparagus isn't quick and you will definitely have a couple of New Year's kisses before fully enjoying lots of fresh spears. Asparagus isn't usually grown from seed – instead you need to buy some 'crowns' (just young asparagus plants) that usually arrive 'bare rooted' (with little to no soil surrounding the roots of the plant – see the photo opposite). Although it is a labour of love, if you can get hold of three-year-old crowns, then you'll be knee-deep in asparagus the following year. Also, just a warning: when your crowns arrive don't scream – they can't help looking like giant spiders.

What you'll need:

- A container or bed that's fairly large – as a guide, one crown would need a 50L (1.3 US gal) pot
- Some rocks/rubble about 3–5cm (1–2in) in diameter
- Multipurpose compost
- Sharp sand (a slightly gritty sand – you can get hold of it at garden centres and builders' merchants)
- Asparagus crowns (I like Crimson Pacific and Gijnlim)
- General liquid feed

SOW

You can do this in early spring or mid-autumn. Place a few rocks in the bottom of your container to help with drainage, mix the compost (80%) with the sand (20%) and fill the container half full. Place one crown in the centre of each 50L (1.3 US gal) container, or space them about 30cm (12in) apart if planting in a bed, then cover with 12cm (5in) of compost. Finally, water them in well and place outside in a warm, sunny spot. Wasn't that easy?

GROW

You need to look after them for the next two years. Feed them every spring with general fertilizer, don't let them dry out, cut back the yellow foliage in autumn and apply well-rotted manure or fresh compost to the container surface once a year in late autumn or winter.

GATHER

It's mid-spring in the second year of growth and you can finally pick some asparagus. Only harvest half the spears in the second year – it's only from the third year that you can collect the full harvest – so don't get carried away. Cut the spears level with the ground at around six inches long. That's it, get cooking, make yourself feel all posh and breathe in the familiar aroma of post-asparagus pee!

TIPS

Fancy making your homegrown asparagus look even stranger? Then why not grow some alien-looking white asparagus? Guess what, it's the same plant! All you have to do is place an upturned container or pot over your asparagus while it's growing to block out the light. Super simple.

FLOWERS

Calabrese

Wild garlic

Borage

Thyme

Courgette

Romanesco

Brussels sprouts

Sprouting broccoli

Nasturtium

Cauliflower

CALABRESE

I'm afraid it's not a gust of high-calorie wind, it's actually broccoli. Another one of these brassicas that we use in our day-to-day cooking that's really simple to grow at home. The head that you eat is a collection of tasty flower buds, all tightly packed together. Originating from Italy and cultivated by the Romans, this fibrous brassica didn't appear in America until the eighteenth century. These plants prefer it cooler, but can grow really well in a small space with lots of light.

What you'll need:
- Seed module tray
- Multipurpose compost
- Calabrese seeds (I like Zen and Kabuki)
- A raised bed or a pot (15–20L/4–5.25 US gal per plant)

SOW

It's mid-spring and your nose has finally defrosted after winter. Grab your seed tray and fill it up with compost. In the centre of each module make a 1cm (½in) deep hole with a pencil or dibber. Drop one seed in each hole and cover with a little more compost. Give them a little tinkle of water and pop on a warm windowsill. Don't let them dry out. Sit back, chew on some other vegetables and watch them grow.

GROW

Once your beautiful broccoli plants are around 10cm (4in) high, you want to get them outside and into their next soil-filled home. Fill up your chosen container or bed and poke some holes big enough to slot in each seedling. You want 60cm (2ft) between each plant (or one plant to each 15–20L/4–5.25 US gal pot) as they will get rather bushy and fill the space. Keep your broccoli plants well watered and get those night-vision goggles on to catch any slugs or snails. Netting your plants will help stop the butterflies laying their eggs and creating a feast for caterpillars.

GATHER

I can't give you exact timings, but if you've kept them watered and protected, then the heads should form at some point after 100 days from sowing – once the heads have reached a size you like, you can cut them off at the stem. Once you've sacrificed your plant to the vegetable gods and cut its head off, then that's usually the end of your broccoli plant. However, if you leave the plant to grow and keep watering it after harvesting the head, it can sometimes produce lots of smaller heads a few weeks later, which are also delicious to eat. Get cooking with that broccoli.

TIPS

Lots of water is key to stopping the plants being stressed, and you can always give them a little liquid feed every couple of weeks.

Want to get more from your plant than just the head? Well, you're in luck, because you can also harvest the broccoli leaves – eat them raw or cook them like spinach leaves.

WILD GARLIC

This is something commonly found in the pocket of foraging foodies or hipsters in cord trousers. It might be wild, it might taste like garlic and it might be super-fashionable for chefs to use, but this stuff is as common as muck and has been around forever. An allium relative and found in shaded woodland and along footpaths in Britain and Europe, it's perfect for a shaded balcony or back garden. Wild garlic has been used since Neolithic times for its herbal and medicinal properties, but if there's one thing you should be aware of it's that wild garlic is really prolific and spreads like wildfire. If you fancy a bit of fresh wild garlic at home, then let's get on with it!

What you'll need:

- A shady bed, or large pot or container
- Multipurpose compost
- Wild garlic bulbs
- Potash (potassium salts)

SOW

You can plant these garlic beauties in autumn or spring, depending on when you order your bulbs. Fill your container almost to the top with compost. You want to plant them 4cm (1½in) deep in small clumps of about six bulbs each. Ensure the clumps are at least 12cm (5in) apart. Make sure the pointy end of each bulb is facing upwards, then cover them with a little more compost. If you've planted them in a pot, pop them in a shady spot outside. The odd rain shower should be enough to keep them happy. Garlic mission complete!

GROW

Keep the container weed-free until the bulbs start to shoot and keep them watered in dry spells. If you've planted in autumn, you'll want to put some potash on the soil surface in late winter/early spring as this will help to feed the garlic as it emerges.

GATHER

Don't get carried away and pick your wild garlic as soon as it appears. You can pick the flowers as and when you want to use them (they're lovely in salads) but wait until the foliage is really full and lush before diving into the leaves. Try making pesto from the leaves or deep-fry the flowers until crisp.

TIPS

Your bulbs will grow year after year but splitting every two to three years will help keep them prolific. To do this, simply dig up the bulbs carefully and pull them apart where you see a natural divide. Replant following the instructions above.

Try not to dig up naturalized bulbs in woodland, as they should be left alone. If you want to top up your homegrown wild garlic harvest then, by all means, go gather more foliage and flowers from your local woodland – just don't pick it near paths as it's probably covered with dog urine!

BORAGE

This isn't the tastiest of edible flowers compared to some of the others in this chapter, but it does add a decent cucumber twang when used to garnish drinks. Like squirrels are attracted to nuts, bees can't get enough of borage and as we all want to have more insects at home this is the perfect plant to try. So, why is it so great? It's colourful, fast-growing and is a prolific self-seeder, so once you've grown borage, you'll always have it. Borage is native to the Mediterranean and has been used medicinally for centuries. The flowers can be eaten as well as the hairy leaves, which are used in soups and with pasta across Europe. If you fancy a bit of borage in your life, then get set and grow.

What you'll need:

- Raised bed, hanging basket, large pot
- Multipurpose compost
- Borage seeds

SOW

You want to sow your borage in early spring, after the last frost. Borage can also be bought as plug plants, but I prefer to grow it from seed as it's so simple and easy. Fill the container you've chosen with compost almost to the top and sparsely sprinkle the seeds on the surface. Cover the seeds with a super-thin layer of compost, water gently and then place indoors or outside in a sunny spot. Sit back and watch your hairy friends grow.

GROW

Apart from watering, borage doesn't need any extra help. It's pretty tough and should grow fast, with flowers forming after seven to eight weeks from sowing.

GATHER

Pick those beautiful blue, pink and white flowers by pinching them off just behind the head, or use some scissors. If you're using the leaves, try not to decimate the plant by chopping all the leaves off at once. Enjoy the huge number of bees on your plants and the cucumber taste on your lips!

TIPS

I like to freeze borage flowers into ice cubes to simultaneously garnish and tart up cocktails.

Don't empty the pot once your borage has died back, as it will be full of seeds for next year. Just pop it to one side and keep it weed free ready for next spring.

THYME

Who doesn't want thyme in their garden? This age-old herb grows happily in containers, but I guess you're wondering why it's in the flower chapter? Funnily enough, for the flowers! As with lots of other edible flowers, they contain a milder flavour than the parent plant.

Now, you can sow thyme seeds if you fancy, but I think it's best to cheat with this one and speed up the process by buying small plug plants and growing them on.

Thyme has been used throughout history in cooking and for medical ailments. In fact, thyme oil (Thymol) is an antiseptic and is commercially used in mouthwash. When it comes to choosing a variety, there are quite a few to consider: common garden, golden, variegated, creeping, lemon… the list goes on. Each have different aromas and growing habits, so choose wisely to suit your space.

What you'll need:

- A container or pot (roughly 10 L/2.6 US gal per plant), or a bed of some description
- Multipurpose compost
- Thyme plug plants (I'd stick with common or a funky variety like Lemon)
- Grit or Gravel

SOW

Fill your chosen container with compost. If planting in a big container or bed, space your plug plants about 25cm (10in) apart. Alternatively, plant up one plug plant per 10L (2.6 US gal) pot. Make a suitably sized hole, pop them in it and give everything a good water. Place in a sunny spot.

GROW

Make sure you don't overwater your thyme plants as they don't like to be swimming. Add some horticultural grit or gravel to the compost surface around each plant to prevent the lower foliage from getting damp.

GATHER

Of course, use the thyme leaves as a herb, but do allow the plant to flower first and give them a try when they appear. After flowering, give your plants a quick trim to remove any dead sections and shape if they've become a mess. Enjoy fresh thyme whenever you want and over time add more plants if needed. Now stop buying packet herbs, please!

TIPS

Bush management is important. Don't go hacking every flower and leaf off your plants like Edward Scissorhands. Selective cutting will help your plants grow successfully for years, so ensure you harvest the thyme in small amounts and from a variety of places on the bush, rather than hacking off huge chunks.

Try drying your own thyme by cutting and bunching up stems with twine, and leaving them to hang up to dry out. Once dry, store in an airtight container in the store cupboard for use during winter months.

COURGETTE (ZUCCHINI)

'Sam, this is not a flower!' I hear you cry. True, but everybody seems to be eating deep-fried courgette flowers stuffed with a heart-attack-inducing amount of cheese these days. Yes, they taste great, but I do think that might have something to do with the cheese…

Courgettes, or zucchini as they're also known, are fast-growing, easy to look after and produce shedloads of edible flowers and fruit throughout the year. It's a member of the cucurbit family (cucumbers, pumpkins, squashes, etc) and, like all cucurbits, it originates from the Americas. It wasn't until the nineteenth century in Italy that zucchini became popular in cooking.

There are so many amazing varieties of courgette you can grow, so say goodbye to plain old green courgettes and check out stripes, yellows, lime greens and two tones! Let's get growing…

What you'll need:

- 7–9cm pots (one per seed)
- Multipurpose compost
- Courgette seeds (my favourites are Zephyr, Sunstripe and Pantheon)
- A large tub, container or bed (ensure you have at least 25L/6.5 US gal of space per plant)

SOW

In early spring, fill your smaller pots with compost, nearly to the top. You want to sow the seeds vertically on their edge, with the pointed tip facing upwards – this is to ensure they don't rot. Grab a seed between your finger and thumb, with pointed end facing towards your hand, then push the seed and your fingers into the compost so it sits 2cm (¾in) below the surface. Cover with a little more compost, water and place on a warm, bright windowsill. Repeat with the rest of your seeds and pots. Keep them well watered but not soaked.

GROW

Once your courgette plants are looking hefty, have grown two to three spiky leaves and are about 15cm (6in) tall, it's time to transplant them into something larger. Fill a 25L (6.5 US gal) container with compost, create a small hole in the centre, then pop one courgette plant into it and push down gently to secure. Repeat with the rest of your plants. If planting your courgette plants in a bed, ensure they're spaced 30–40cm (12–16in) apart. Give all the plants a good water. You can grow courgettes inside near French doors or a large window where there's lots of light. Otherwise, keep them in a sunny spot outdoors. Keep them well watered and for an extra boost add general fertilizer to the compost surface. Now watch them grow fast.

GATHER

As soon as you see the flowers forming you can start harvesting. Being careful not to damage the main plant, gently cut each mini flowering courgette off the base of the plant with a sharp knife, then you can carefully cut the flower from the mini courgette. The more you pick the more they will produce as they start to engulf the space in which they're growing. Mini courgettes are delicious, but if you prefer a slightly larger fruit, then simply leave them on the plant until they're at the desired size.

TIPS

Regular watering will help prevent rot forming on the tips of the fruits.

ROMANESCO

This might sound like a good name for a rapper, but it's still just a vegetable, a brilliant one though. Whoever thought up the crazy flower pattern for this cauliflower relative is a genius. On top of their appearance, their flavour is awesome as well, which is why I prefer them over their white relative. Yep, they're related to cauliflowers, have been around in Italy since the sixteenth century and are classed as an heirloom variety. Despite its heritage, it seems fairly new to the veg-patch scene and wasn't commercially available across Europe and America until the 1990s. If you're fed up with cauliflowers and want something to impress your dinner guests, then get growing and cook up a right big Romanesco storm!

What you'll need:
- Seed module tray
- Multipurpose compost
- Romanesco seeds (give Navona a try if you can find it, although most are sold without a variety name)
- Large container or raised bed

SOW

Similar to growing cauliflowers, seed sowing should be done from mid-spring. Fill your seed tray with compost. Make a 1cm (½in) deep hole in the middle of each cell with your finger or a dibber. Pop one seed in each, cover over with a little more compost, then give them a dribble of water. Keep the compost damp, pop them on a warm windowsill and let them grow.

GROW

Once those baby Romanesco plants are around 10cm (4in) high you can plant them out in their final spot. You'll need to leave roughly 60cm (2ft) between each plant if placing them in a bed, so don't ram them in. If potting in a container, you'll need a 10–15L (2.5–4 US gal) pot per plant. Create a hole large enough to fit your seedling, pop it in, then gently press down on the compost around the base of the plant to make sure it's secure. Keep the plants well watered in a sunny spot.

GATHER

Around 90 days after planting out your seedlings, a tight geometric head should start to form. Sometimes you'll get a 'split head', but the result will still be delicious. Once the heads have reached a good size, cut them off at the stem and enjoy. Just like broccoli, the plant will regrow some mini florets after harvest, but these are normally too small to bother with.

TIPS

I recommend hunting high and low for a white variety called De Jesi, which is super-nutty and something a bit special.

Net your plants to stop the butterflies and caterpillars from happily attacking them. It's also worth checking your plants regularly and picking of any caterpillars that might be lurking on them.

BRUSSELS SPROUTS

To some, Brussels sprouts are the worst-tasting thing they've ever had in their mouth; to others, a great tasting winter vegetable commonly associated with Christmas. Personally, I love them, and the peculiar way in which they grow just adds to their charm. Part of the cabbage family, they grow tall and upright, with the sprouts forming on the sides of a thick stem. The sprouts are immature flower buds, tucked up into tight balls, which, after consuming, will leave you with a good deal of wind. They first arrived in Europe around the fifth century and a few centuries later they were cultivated in (not surprisingly) Brussels, in Belgium. Since then, hybrids have been created to reduce the bitterness and produce some beautiful red and purple varieties. Get growing and may the flatulence be with you!

What you'll need:
- A 15L (4 US gal) container per plant, or seed module tray and a raised bed
- Multipurpose compost
- Sprout seeds (I love Red Bull and Brigitte)

SOW

Sow in early spring. If you're growing in movable 15L (4 US gal) pots, then fill them with compost nearly to the top. In the centre of each pot make a 1cm (½in) deep hole with a finger or dibber, then pop a seed in the hole. Cover with a little more compost and give them a careful water. Repeat with the rest of your seeds and pots, then leave in a sunny spot indoors. If you plan to grow them in a raised bed, then sow your seeds in a seed module tray first. Fill the module tray with compost, create a 1cm (½in) deep hole in each cell as above, then add a seed to each one, cover with a little compost and water gently. Place on a warm, bright windowsill and don't let them dry out. Move them outside once they are 7–10cm (3–4in) high. If you want lots of plants in a larger bed, then use the same method but in a seed tray and then transplant into their final spot once they are a few inches high. Grow sprouts, grow!

GROW

Once the seedlings are 7–10cm (3–4in) tall, move them outside. If you're planting into a raised bed, make small holes in the bed 20cm (8in) apart, then remove the seedlings from the seed module tray and pop a seedling into each hole. Keep them well watered and net your plants if they're attracting a lot of butterflies. If your stems become a bit floppy you can add some support in the form of bamboo sticks, or gently tie the plants to a wall or railings. Sit back and watch those stems grow.

GATHER

Your Brussels sprouts won't be ready to harvest until late autumn or early winter. If you can, allow your sprout plants to experience a frost before harvesting them – this helps to increase the sugars in the plant, therefore, reducing the bitterness of your veg. Pick your sprouts when they're a little smaller than a ping pong ball by cutting each one off the stem with a sharp knife. By just removing individual sprouts rather than the whole stem, the plant should produce more sprouts for you.

TIPS

Try feeding your sprout plants throughout the season with a general liquid fertilizer and by adding chicken pellets to the soil surface around the plants.

Bored of eating them boiled? Try finely slicing and frying them in butter with a bit of smoked bacon, or with anything else you've got in your growing space.

SPROUTING BROCCOLI

This is another type of flower bud and a close relative of calabrese (broccoli), but with a longer stem and a purple top, hence why it's commonly called purple sprouting broccoli (PSB). You'll be pleased to hear, however, that it's also now available in white varieties, which is my favourite. If you've never grown sprouting broccoli, then you're in for a treat, as not only do you get tons to eat but they can produce florets over many weeks with careful care. Historically, these plants were giants, growing to around 1.5m (5ft) in height, appeared in many colours from green, red and brown, and everything on the plant was eaten. Brought to Europe from the eastern Mediterranean, it's now grown across the world in a less gigantic form. Make sure you give the leaves a try as they have a particularly lovely mild-mustard hit.

What you'll need:
- Seed module tray
- Multipurpose compost
- Sprouting broccoli seeds (for a purple variety try Cardinal; for a white variety try Burbank)
- 15–20L (4–5.25 US gal) pots or containers (one for each plant), or a raised bed

SOW

Sowing should be done from mid-spring to midsummer. Grab your seed tray, fill it with compost and make a 1cm (½in) deep hole with your finger or a dibber in the centre of each cell. Pop one seed in each hole and cover over with a little more compost, followed by a little watering. Keep them on a warm windowsill and let them grow. Don't let them dry out.

GROW

Once those young 'sproutlings' are around 10cm (4in) high you can plant them outside in their final container. Fill up your chosen container or bed with compost and poke some holes big enough to slot in each seedling. You want 60cm (2ft) between each plant (or one plant to each 15–20L/4–5.25 US gal pot) as they will get rather bushy and fill the space. Keep your broccoli plants well watered and watch out for slugs, snails and butterflies. Netting your plants will help stop the butterflies in their tracks!

GATHER

Most varieties will take seven to eight months from sowing before you can harvest. At this stage, you should have a giant brassica bush that any grower would be proud of and in the centre of it you will see the head forming. Now, there are two ways to harvest. The first is to let this centre grow a little and then harvest once it's a few centimetres/inches long. The other method is to let a decent-sized head form (about the size of a cricket ball or baseball), cut it right out at the stem (eat it), then wait for the plant to put all its energy into growing long side florets, which you'll recognize more as sprouting broccoli. Don't neglect your plants after the first harvest, as they will keep producing edible sprouting goodness that you can include in your five-a-day for several weeks if you keep them watered and pest-free.

TIPS

Be on high alert for slugs, snails and butterflies/caterpillars. Use the beer traps (page 25) and nets to keep your plants looking as well groomed as my beard!

NASTURTIUM

'Sam, it's about time you actually mentioned a proper flower in this chapter!'

I'm going to be honest with you, I hate people going on about putting flowers on everything they eat because it looks pretty. I only want to eat flowers if they add flavour to a dish and attract lots of insects to my garden. Luckily, nasturtium plants tick both those boxes. Nasturtiums have tasty flowers and leaves, both giving a mild peppery zing to any dish, and the bright orange flowers also attract butterflies (especially ones that eat brassicas), bees and many other flying insects. Having nasturtiums helps with pollination as well as being a distraction to unwanted insects from our other plants (e.g. the brassicas). Originating from Central/South America, this colourful annual arrived in Europe via Spain in the late sixteenth century. They really are a brilliant edible flower to grow and one to get children involved with. And don't forget to tell them that its Latin name translates as 'nose-twister' or 'nose-tweaker'.

What you'll need:

- Small pots, window box or raised bed… basically, anything
- Multipurpose compost
- Nasturtium seeds (I like Ladybird, or give a climbing variety like Indian Cress a try)

SOW

Get sowing your packet of seeds in spring. If sowing directly outside, then wait until after the final frost, although these do germinate really well indoors, so I recommend starting them off inside. Fill your chosen container with compost to 2.5cm (1in) from the top and sparsely scatter some seeds over the surface of the soil. Cover them with 2cm (¾in) of compost, water gently, then put them somewhere light and warm. Wasn't that simple?

GROW

Keep your plants well watered but not drenched as they prefer not to sit in water. Once they are 5cm (2in) tall, move them outside to a sunny spot. Nasturtiums like to trail, so place them on a window ledge, balcony or wall to allow them to hang prettily – this also means they're great for growing if you're short on space. Like my grandad, they love a good ramble!

GATHER

You'll have tons of flowers three months from sowing. The more flowers you pick, the more they produce. Like people, all plants want to do is reproduce, and so by removing the flowers they produce more and more. When you're not admiring their lovely blooms, use the peppery leaves and flowers in salads.

TIPS

If you love capers and want to try an alternative, give nasturtium seed pods a try. These are often called 'poor man's capers', but they are far from poor in flavour! Let your flowers go to seed and carefully pick off the unripe pods. Pickle them in a brine mix (have a look online for a recipe) and pop them in a jar in the fridge. I actually prefer these peppery balls to the real McCoy.

CAULIFLOWER

Whether you love the humble cauliflower bathed in cheese, boiled within an inch of its life, or as a tasty vegan 'steak', then you'll want to grow some at home.

I always find there's something quite beautiful about this pristine brain-shaped flower unwrapping itself in the garden… well, until I come along and cut its head off! As its name suggests it's a flower or, to be more precise, a clump of flower buds, which is the same for a lot of brassicas like broccoli, sprouts, etc. Introduced into Europe around the sixteenth century, although not appearing in America until the 1900s, this vegetable would have had a much smaller head originally to the one we know and love today. If you're not already desperate to whip off your slippers and start sowing, you'll be pleased to know that cauliflowers are also available in some mind-bending psychedelic colours like purple, orange, yellow and green.

What you'll need:

- Seed module tray
- Multipurpose compost
- Cauliflower seeds (give a purple variety like Graffiti a try)
- A raised bed or pots (15–20L/4–5.25 US gal per plant)

SOW

In early- to mid-spring fill your seed tray with compost. With a small pencil, dibber or your finger, make a 1cm (½in) deep hole in each cell and pop one seed in each. Fill in the holes with a little more compost and give them a gentle water. Pop them somewhere warm and bright, like a windowsill, and leave to germinate. Don't let them dry out.

GROW

Once the seedlings are around 10cm (4in) tall, you can plant them out in their final position. Fill up your chosen container or bed with compost and poke some holes big enough to slot in each seedling. You want 60cm (2ft) between each plant (or one plant to each 15–20L/4–5.25 US gal pot) as they will get rather bushy and fill the space. Keep your cauliflower plants well watered and watch out for slugs, snails and butterflies. Netting your plants will help stop the butterflies in their tracks. If your house is on the cooler side and has enough natural light, then you can grow these inside, although you'll have to deal with the cabbagey smell all day, every day. Make sure you keep your plants well watered.

GATHER

After three to five months, your cauliflower is ready to harvest (although it's pretty simple to tell when a cauliflower is ready, as a big head will have formed under the leaves). Harvest when it's at the size you want, and still looking vibrant, by cutting at the base of the stem with a sharp knife. You may end up with smaller heads than you'd ideally like, which happens if the cauliflowers weren't completely happy while growing, but just remember it's not all about the size. Battered cauliflower anyone?

TIPS

Cauliflowers are like narcotics to butterflies, caterpillars, slugs and snails! You need to protect the plants with whatever arsenal you can come up with. Nets, beer traps and even lifting them off the ground will help keep your plants looking beautiful and undamaged.

If you can get hold of some manure, then put a bit in the bottom of your containers or bed before you add the compost, as it will really help speed up the growth process of your cauliflowers.

LEAVES

Parsley

Kale

Spinach

Mixed baby salad

Chard

Mint

Napa cabbage

Lettuce

Basil

Kalettes

Traditional cabbage

PARSLEY

Here's another herb commonly found needlessly wrapped in plastic on a supermarket shelf. It's considered boring by many, but I very much disagree with this. So, flat or curly? I'm not talking about chest hair or your favourite dog breed, but the two types of parsley that are grown and consumed across the globe. I don't think there is much difference in taste when you compare the two – it's more about texture. For something with more bite to it go for curly, whereas flat parsley is much better for chopping and combining with other ingredients. Either way, parsley sauce is something that brings back fond memories of my childhood, although I think the fond memories might have something to do with the mountain of mashed potato that was served with it.

Historically, parsley was considered to be more holy than the Pope – all stemming from some Greek dude, a few angry serpents and parsley growing from his blood! With that in mind, it makes sense that it originates from the Mediterranean and was being cultivated as early as the third century BCE. As with many herbs, growing parsley from seed is slow and not always successful (it can take four to six weeks to germinate), so I always recommend buying plug plants instead.

I think everyone should have this leafy herb growing at home, so grab a pot, order a plug plant and get growing.

What you'll need:

- Medium pot or window box (anything really that will hold compost)
- Multipurpose compost
- Parsley plug plants

SOW

Buy and sow parsley plug plants from mid-spring onwards. Fill up your chosen container with compost nearly to the top. With your hands or a small trowel/spade make small holes for each of your plants, spaced roughly about 10cm (4in) apart. Carefully pop a plant into each hole, press in gently with your hands, then give them a decent dose of water. Keep them outside, watered and watch them bush up.

GROW

So, you've now realized how simple growing parsley is, but you still need to keep an eye on it to ensure it doesn't dry out and/or suffer from too much slug/snail action. Apart from that, sharpen those scissors and get the mashed potato ready.

GATHER

Pick your fresh parsley as and when you need it, but as with lots of leafy greens, take the outer leaves off first and try not to cut out the centre leaves that are forming.

TIPS

Parsley is a biennial, which means it takes two years to flower and go to seed, so don't go throwing them out after their first year of growth as they will die back over winter and return the following year.

A general liquid feed once a month will really help to keep your plants growing, especially if you're cutting it every day.

KALE

Not more greens! Well yes, you're in the 'Leaves' chapter. Kale is brilliant and I'm not talking about that stuff you find in shops that's been through a woodchipper and thrown into a plastic bag. That stuff is a poor representation of the wonderful world of kale and all the stunning colours and shapes that are available. You can get pinks, reds, purples, whites along with the common green varieties like curly and cavolo nero. Kale was around long before celebrity fitness influencers were blending it into gross-coloured smoothies. It was, in fact, cultivated in the Eastern Mediterranean around 4,000 years ago and has since spread across the world. Don't be fooled by the mention of Mediterranean climates as this stuff is no bikini-wearing sun lover. It can continue to grow in temperatures as low as -15°C (5°F) and is perfect for growing over winter.

What you'll need:
- Seed module tray
- Multipurpose compost
- Kale seeds (I love Cavolo Nero or Buttonhole)
- Raised bed or 15–20L (4–5.25 US gal) pots (one per plant)

SOW

Check what your seed packet advises, but sowing from mid-spring onwards is fine, and early summer sowings will last all winter. Grab your seed tray and fill it up with compost so it's packed in nice and firm. In the centre of each cell make a 1cm (½in) deep hole with your finger, pencil or dibber. Drop one seed in each hole, then cover with a little compost. Give them a light spray of water and pop on a warm windowsill. Don't let them dry out. Sit back and plan your next seeds to sow.

GROW

Wait until your kale plants are around 10cm (4in) high and then get them outside and into their final growing location. Fill up your chosen container or bed with compost and create some appropriately sized holes for each plant. You want roughly 18cm (7in) between each plant as they will easily fill the space and form a thick kale hedge. As with other brassicas, if you are planting into pots, then you'll need a 15–20L (4–5.25 US gal) pot per plant. Keep your plants well watered and don't forget to go hunting late at night for pests like slugs or snails. Netting your plants will help stop the butterflies trying to procreate on your leaves.

GATHER

When it's ready, it's ready, but this will probably be around three to four months from sowing. Once a head has formed, you can cut the whole thing away from the stem and you'll have a lovely kale rosette. This works great for varieties like Buttonhole, but it will kill the plant and, therefore, mean you only get one harvest from each. The best way to harvest your kale is to keep removing the lower outer leaves as they grow, allowing the centres to keep forming and growing, giving you an endless supply of greens. There's no need for scissors as you can grab each leaf and carefully pull downwards towards the ground – they should make a satisfying crack and pop off. Enjoy your kale forest, get cooking and never buy shredded kale again.

TIPS

Boiling kale is boring and it also sucks all the nutrients out of the plant. Try grilling it for a crispy snack, add it to a tart or chuck it in a stir-fry for a tasty crunch.

Like lots of brassicas (cauliflower, sprouts), kale becomes sweeter after it has had a tickle from Jack Frost, so don't worry about protecting it in the colder months.

SPINACH

'I'm strong to the finish, cause I eats me spinach, I'm Popeye the sailor man!' I'm pretty sure that's the first thing that comes to mind for everyone when someone mentions spinach, right?

Growing up in a Greek household, I became a lover of spinach at an early age, especially when it's combined with pastry and cheese in dishes like spanakopita and tiropitas. So, what's so special about spinach? Well, Popeye was really onto something – a study in 2011 discovered that spinach does, in fact, make you stronger and it's also a great plant to hydrate yourself with as its 91 per cent water. Spinach originates from Asia and we now grow over 26 million tons of the stuff every year.

You get two types of spinach: the 'standard' one, which is an annual, and 'perpetual' spinach, which is a biennial. If you live in a cooler climate, then stick with annual spinach, but if you struggle with really hot conditions, then perpetual spinach will be the one for you as it rarely goes to seed in the first year. Either way, fire up the juicer and get ready for a spinach smoothie… or not.

What you'll need:

- Any medium container you have to hand, window box or raised bed
- Multipurpose compost
- Spinach seeds (try F1 Banjo or El Real)

SOW

You can sow spinach all year round, depending on the variety (check the seed packet), but it will be easier to sow from early spring through to late summer. Fill your pot or container with compost until it's 5cm (2in) from the top and compress it with your hands slightly so that it's not 'loose'. Liberally sprinkle your chosen spinach seeds over the surface of the compost, then cover with another 2.5cm (1in) of compost, water gently and pop in a warm sunny spot, indoors or outside. That was simple, right?

GROW

Keep well watered and once the seeds germinate make sure you move them outside so they don't get too hot. Watch out for slugs and snails and pick off any that are trying to attack your seedlings. If you want smaller plants (i.e. baby spinach leaves), then leave your container to form a thick spinach bush that even Popeye would be proud of. If you want larger plants and, therefore, larger leaves, then thin them out to give a bit more space as they grow. To do this, carefully pinch out and discard all but one seedling every 5cm (2in), so that the remaining spinach plants have space to bush out.

GATHER

Summer varieties should be ready to pick from late spring/early summer, but just keep an eye on them and carefully pick the leaves as and when you need them.

TIPS

Mix a small amount of general fertilizer into the compost before sowing if you want to give your spinach an extra boost. Water them like you're trying to keep Aquaman all shiny and wet as they really don't like to be dry – they'll bolt and flower if they get too thirsty.

MIXED BABY SALAD

Salad leaves are probably the easiest thing you can grow at home, and will thrive in pretty much any container that holds compost. Perfectly happy growing inside in bright light or filling a window box, there is no excuse not to get sowing. Most seed packets labelled as 'mixed salad leaves' or 'mixed baby salad' will contain a variety of different seeds and each brand's mix will differ. The names of the mixes will vary, but look for the varieties included (on the back of the seed packet) and give a mix a try. The great thing about baby salad is that you can sow them in succession in lots of pots all year round and keep cutting from your plants over and over again. So, tell the shops to shove that sweaty plastic-wrapped salad, because you're growing your own at home!

What you'll need:

- Pots, window box, hanging basket – literally anything that will hold compost (I've been known to cut the side off an old milk carton and use that to grow lettuce in)
- Multipurpose compost
- Mixed lettuce leaf seeds (I love Mizuna mix and Mesclun mix)

SOW

You can sow your seeds at any time of year but I would recommend beginning sowing in early spring. I prefer raising my salad off the ground, which helps with pests, so I often opt for sowing in a hanging basket (which is a great space saver too). Fill your chosen container with compost so it's about 2.5cm (1in) from the top. Sprinkle your seeds thinly across the surface of the compost (you want them to be pretty close together). Cover with a thin layer of compost and gently squash it down with your hands. Give it a little water, keep them indoors in a warm spot and let the germinating begin. Don't let them dry out.

GROW

When the seedlings are a couple of centimetres high it's time to move them outside. You'll need to harden them off, which just means getting them used to the temperature outside. Do this by placing them outside during the day and then bringing them back inside at night. Do this for at least a couple of days and then leave them outside for good. Keep them well watered as lettuce plants don't like to be dry. Sit back a watch that salad grow.

GATHER

Who wants a salad party? Just me, okay! There's no perfect time to harvest your leaves, but I find it's best to cut the leaves when they are 7–10cm (3–4in) high (much like the size of leaves you'd find in shop-bought bagged salad). Just go along with a pair of scissors, snipping off however much you need. Try not to cut out the very centre of each salad plant (called the 'growing tip') as once this is snipped off, they will struggle to grow more tasty leaves. If you're careful, you'll be harvesting salad leaves for weeks.

TIPS

Make your own salad mixes by buying your favourite individual lettuce seed packets and mixing them together before sowing. Don't forget to repeat the seed sowing every few weeks so you don't run out of fresh salad leaves.

CHARD

This is not chard, its easy...! Chard, Swiss chard, rainbow chard, leaf beet, silver beet. This is such a colourful leafy vegetable with varieties coming in reds, pinks, yellows, oranges and whites. It can be grown in a pot at home either for the stem, leaf or both. It has been around for centuries, and the name 'chard' comes from the French *carde* and the Latin *carduus* meaning artichoke or cardoon. It's a native of Southern Europe and probably developed from wild beets centuries ago. It likes full sun but is really happy with cooler weather and, therefore, can be sown in early spring and then sown again in early summer – providing you with greens into the following spring. Go grab some chard seeds and get sowing.

What you'll need:
- Large container or raised bed
- Multipurpose compost
- Chard seeds (give Bright Lights and Peppermint a try)

SOW

You can sow chard from early spring but I recommend waiting until mid-spring, as the warmer weather helps with germination. Fill up your bed or container with compost so it's nearly full and then use a pencil, finger or a dibber to 'draw' 2cm (¾in) deep lines in the compost, 30cm (1ft) apart. Sprinkle seeds thinly into each groove, then cover with 2cm (¾in) of compost. If you want to go a bit wild, then just scatter some seeds evenly in your container and cover with 2cm (¾in) of compost. Give them a quick water and place outside in a bright spot (they can get too warm if kept indoors). Don't let them dry out.

GROW

Once your seedlings are a few centimetres/inches high, you can thin the plants out if they start to look a little crowded. To do this, carefully pinch out and discard all but one seedling about every 5cm (2in). Ensure your chard plants are kept damp, especially in the summer.

GATHER

Your chard is ready for harvesting as soon as the plants are established and are at least 45–50cm (18–20in) tall. Cut the outer leaves and stems at the base with a sharp knife, but leave the centre tip alone so that you get continuous growth. Who doesn't love rainbow-coloured food?

TIPS

Cook the stems and leaves separately. Treat the leaves like you would spinach, and slice and fry the stems with a little oil and garlic. Make sure you sow a second batch of seeds later in the year (around early summer) following the instructions above, so you can eat fresh chard over winter and through until the following spring.

MINT

We were mint to be together! Mint is a game changer for fresh breath and it's pretty impressive when you think about how many everyday items contain it: toothpaste, air fresheners, gum, cosmetics, essential oils – the list goes on. Mint can be found across the world and is really happy in moist, damp soil. It will spread like crazy if given the opportunity, so it's important to keep this one confined to a pot, rather than planting it directly into your garden or a raised bed.

There are loads of varieties to choose from: standard garden mint (what we'd typically think of as mint), pineapple mint, peppermint, lemon mint, grapefruit mint, chocolate mint, Moroccan mint, apple mint... Growing mint from seed isn't commonly done, for two reasons. Firstly, some plants are sterile and, therefore, the seeds won't germinate and secondly, mint seeds won't always produce a direct copy of the parent plant. It's always best to buy small plug plants as I describe below, although you can take cuttings from an established bush, or even use a bunch of shop-bought mint, to propagate a mint plant (see TIPS below).

What you'll need:
- A large container (do not plant this directly into a bed)
- Multipurpose compost
- Mint plug plants (try grapefruit or garden)

SOW

From around mid-spring, get hold of some decent mint plug plants. Fill up your large chosen container with compost – I've seen mint grow pretty much everywhere, so as long as it's got enough space for it to bush out and you keep it wet, you don't need to worry too much about what container you use. Create small holes in the compost big enough for your plug plants, around 10cm (4in) apart, and pop a plant into each. Give them a really good water and keep them outside in a sunny spot!

GROW

Don't let them dry out – in this case over-watering won't harm them. If you've decided to sow more than one variety, make sure the containers aren't near each other as otherwise they will lose their lovely individual flavour and scent. Your mint plants should last for years – if your container becomes over-crowded after a few years, then gently dig up the plants, split them by carefully pulling apart the roots and stems, then replant a few of them into your container. Plant the remaining plants into new pots, or give them away to friends.

GATHER

Don't go cutting all the mint off like an angry samurai as you'll cause the plant to struggle, especially in the first year of growth. Careful pruning as and when you need it will be much better for the plant. You're now a master of all things minty!

TIPS

Give it some invest-mint and make sure you have a large enough, permanent container for it to spread and produce usable mint year after year.

If you want to grow mint from cuttings, then place the stems in a glass or jar of water. Replace the water every couple of days until roots appear at the base of the stems. Once you have roots, plant the mint into small compost-filled pots and keep them well watered in a bright spot. Transplant them into a large container when they look big enough, following the instructions above. Simple!

NAPA CABBAGE

Although growing them uses the exact same methods as traditional cabbage, I just had to include napa cabbage in this chapter, especially when they have the Latin name *Brassica rapa* – innit blud! They're also known as Chinese cabbage as they originated from China in the fifteenth century. These are the bees knees when it comes to cabbages, with their funky barrel shape and beautiful colours. They have a lettuce-like crispness that makes them a versatile vegetable in the kitchen and they mature slowly, so there's no need to eat cabbage every night. If there's one brassica you should grow at home, it's this.

What you'll need:

- Seed module tray
- Multipurpose compost
- Napa cabbage seeds (give the red Scarvita or green Yuki a go)
- Large pot or container for one or more plants

SOW

You can sow seeds from mid-spring, but the plants prefer the slightly cooler weather of autumn as they mature, so I find a midsummer sowing is best. Fill your seed tray with compost. Make a 1cm (½in) deep hole in each cell with a pencil, finger or dibber. Pop one seed in each, cover with a little compost and give them a little water. Keep them damp on a warm windowsill.

GROW

When your napas are around 10cm (4in) tall you can plant them out where they're going to live. They need less space than traditional cabbages – 30cm (1ft) between each plant is ideal if planting into a raised bed – otherwise you'll need a 10L (2.6 US gal) pot per plant. Create small holes with a trowel or your hands, big enough for your baby cabbages, then pop one into each hole. Secure by gently pressing down with your hands at the base of the plant, then water them well. They don't seem to be as smelly as traditional cabbages, so you can grow them indoors near a bright window, but I recommend keeping them outside in a sunny spot. Keep them well watered when the weather is warm and dry, but don't soak them.

GATHER

Your napa cabbages should be ready to harvest around 80 days after sowing, but this can vary a bit. Once you have a well-formed tower-shaped head, cut it off cleanly at the stem using a sharp knife.

TIPS

Don't take a nap-a! If you're not falling asleep at the thought of growing cabbages, then I urge you to give this one a go – it's great shredded into stir-fries or for making into kimchi. Like all brassicas, butterflies will be after these guys, so definitely protect your plants with some insect netting if you can, or keep an eye out for caterpillars and pick them off when you see them.

LETTUCE

When asked what my favourite meal was when I was little, I would always answer 'lettuce'. Yep, that's right. I still love it, but only my homegrown leaves, and here's why. Over 50 per cent of bagged salad sold in shops is grown in China, it's then packed into non-recyclable bags and shipped around the world. What's more, you just get a few sad leaves that lack in flavour. I urge you not to buy bagged lettuce unless it's grown in your home country and packaged in recyclable or compostable packaging.

Growing your own is not only better in terms of flavour and food miles, but you're also growing the entire head of lettuce, so it's greater value for money.

There are so many different varieties of lettuce available, each with different flavours and colours, and growing them at home couldn't be easier. We've been eating lettuce like rabbits for centuries, and it was first farmed by the ancient Egyptians, but it wasn't until the eighteenth century that many of the varieties appeared that we enjoy growing and eating today.

What you'll need:

- Seed module tray
- Multipurpose compost
- Lettuce seeds (I love Oakleaf and Lollo rosso)
- Pot, window box – any medium to large container

SOW

Lettuce can be sowed from early spring until late summer, and if you want salad with every meal, then sow some lettuce seeds every two to three weeks. You need to sow into seed module trays first and then transplant. Fill your seed trays with compost nearly to the top, then thinly scatter one or two seeds across the surface of each cell. Cover with a fine layer of compost, give them a gentle water and pop somewhere warm. Pretty simple, right?

GROW

Keep your plants well watered. Once your seedlings are big enough to carefully handle you need to thin them out. This means removing some of your germinated seedlings to give the others room to grow. You want to pinch out carefully with your fingers and discard excess seedlings, leaving just one plant per module. Once the lettuces are around 8cm (3in) high, fill up your chosen container and create small holes 20cm (8in) apart, using a trowel or your hands. Pop a baby lettuce into each hole and gently press down around the base to secure.

Growing them indoors will cause them to bolt (not form a head) and flower, which we don't want, so place your lettuce plants outside in a sunny spot.

GATHER

You can pick individual outer leaves from around seven weeks after sowing, but we want the heads to eat. Your plants should form heads after around 10 weeks from sowing. At this stage, use a sharp knife to cut them from the stem – give them a wash and enjoy delicious homegrown salads. The stems may resprout, but usually you'll have to sow more seeds and repeat the above process for a second crop.

TIPS

Feel free to buy lettuce plugs and plant them out into your container – its quicker and works just as well. You will need to protect your lettuce plants from being attacked by slugs and snails – I find lifting my container off the ground using bricks, or planting into a hanging basket or window box, helps. Also consider the trusty beer traps (see page 25).

BASIL

Instead of buying plastic-wrapped basil from a shop, try growing some at home – it's a super-smelling annual herb that goes great in almost everything. Sweet or Italian basil is the standard variety you'll find in supermarkets, but by growing at home from seed you can get your hands on some great-tasting varieties like bush, purple, cinnamon, lemon, plus many more. We've been using basil leaves medicinally and in our food for over 5,000 years, and it seems to have originated from North Africa, India and Southeast Asia, but can now be found growing globally. Once you've tried homegrown basil, I promise you'll never go back to store-bought.

What you'll need:

- A medium pot or container
- Multipurpose compost
- Basil seeds (give Dolly or Shiraz a whirl)
- A clear plastic bag big enough to cover your pot (like a freezer bag)

SOW

You can start sowing basil from early spring and until late summer. Grab your chosen pot and fill it with compost, 2.5cm (1in) from the top. Sprinkle some seeds sparingly onto the surface of your compost, then cover them with another fine layer of compost. Give them a gentle water and then place the bag over the top of the pot – this acts as a mini greenhouse, keeping the environment warm and humid to allow the seeds to germinate. Pop them in a warm spot and wait for the magic to happen. Give them a spritz of water every now and then if they look like they're drying out.

GROW

Keep checking your pot, and as soon as you see that the seeds have germinated remove the plastic bag. For a decent bush with lots of leaves grow your basil in a sunny spot indoors. They'll also happily live outside, but the more heat you can provide the better (if you have a mini greenhouse or polytunnel, they'll love it in there). Keep them watered but not soaked, sing some Italian opera and pinch out the central growing tips to encourage them to bush out.

GATHER

After around 50 days from sowing, the warmth, watering and pinching out should have paid off and you should be the proud owner of a very bushy basil plant. Carefully and evenly pick the leaves and tips as and when you need them, or you can harvest a whole plant at once if you've got more on the way.

TIPS

Make sure you remove any flowers that appear as they slow down the growth of the plant. Basil plants are best buddies with tomatoes, so grow them next to each other in the same container if you can. If you go bonkers for basil and want an endless supply, then try sowing in succession every two to three weeks.

KALETTES

Also known as 'flower sprouts' or 'kale sprouts', kalettes are essentially a Brussels sprout stem with some better-tasting kale flowers emerging instead. Clearly, someone loved sprouts and kale so much that they decided to combine the two. They were developed in the UK, after several years of careful cross-breeding between Brussel sprouts and kale, which sounds a bit mad, but when you see all these little rosettes covering a sprout stem, they look ace. On top of all that they are easy to grow and, in my opinion, taste awesome. They appeared commercially in 2010. You might have seen these little guys bagged up in the shops, but trust me when I tell you that they taste far better when homegrown.

What you'll need:
- A 15L (4 US gal) pot per plant, or a raised bed
- Multipurpose compost
- Seed module tray (optional)
- Kalette seeds

SOW

You can sow kalettes at the same time as you sow your regular sprouts from early spring onwards. Fill your chosen pot(s) with compost nearly to the top. In the centre of each pot make a 1cm (½in) deep hole with your finger, pop one seed in, cover with a little more compost and give them a gentle water. If you plan to grow them in a raised bed, then sow your seeds in a seed module tray first. Fill the module tray with compost, create a 1cm (½in) deep hole in each cell as above, adding a seed to each, cover with a little compost and water gently. Keep them inside in a warm sunny spot and don't let them dry out.

GROW

Once the seedlings are 8–10cm (3–4in) tall, move them outside. If you're planting into a raised bed, make small holes in the bed 30cm (1ft) apart, then pop a seedling from the seed module tray into each hole. Keep them well watered and net your plants if they're attracting a lot of butterflies. If your stem becomes a bit floppy you can add some support in the form of bamboo sticks, or gently tie the plants to a wall or railings.

GATHER

Your plants should be ready to harvest from late autumn/early winter. You can either harvest individual kalettes as and when you need them by cutting them off the stem with a sharp knife, or you can cut the entire stem off at the base of the plant and wave it round like a kalette-growing Jedi. Boil them, fry them or – my favourite way – grill them.

TIPS

The same as you would with sprouts (page 97), try feeding your kalette plants throughout the season with a general liquid feed and add chicken pellets to the soil surface in summer.

You can boil, fry, steam or grill kalettes – I also like to barbecue them with a little oil and salt and pepper for a crispy winter snack.

TRADITIONAL CABBAGE

Trying to tell someone how great cabbages are is just as hard as trying to tell my late and much-loved Greek nan that chicken is not fine to put in a vegetarian soup. Honestly though, cabbages are pretty cool, and you can grow lots of different types and colours. Cabbages have been around for ages and their origins are mostly unknown – one of the first mentions of them was in the fourteenth century when they were noted as being a food for peasants in Britain and Western Europe. Fast forward to the present day and cabbages are eaten by everyone across the world. You can get giant (the world record is a crazy 62.7kg/138.3lb), pointed, red and even pink cabbages. I know it's divisive, but I personally can't get enough of that cabbage aroma in my garden. Why not give it a go? Who knows, you might even grow your own world-record-beating beast!

What you'll need:

- Seed module tray
- Multipurpose compost
- Cabbage seeds (I'd try January King or Rodima)
- 15–20L (4–5.25 US gal) pot per plant, or larger container for multiple plants

SOW

Similar to growing any other brassica, sowing can be done from mid-spring onwards. Fill your seed tray with compost, making a 1cm (½in) deep hole with a finger, dibber or pencil in the centre of each cell. Pop one seed in each, cover with a little more compost and give them all a dribble of water. Keep them on a warm windowsill and let the cabbage carnival commence. Don't let them dry out.

GROW

Once you have some little cabbage plants that are around 10cm (4in) tall, you can plant them out in their final container or bed. They need roughly 60cm (2ft) between each plant if planting in a raised bed, so don't squash them in like sardines. If you're transplanting them into pots, then you'll need a 15–20L (4–5.25 US gal) pot per plant. Fill your chosen container with compost and make small holes just big enough for your baby cabbages. Pop a plant into each hole and secure by gently pressing around its base with your hands. Keep well watered outside in a sunny spot. Watch out for butterflies and protect your plants with some insect netting.

GATHER

The official time it takes a cabbage to mature from transplanting is 60–100 days, but just use your eyes and look for the head as it forms. Once it's reached a size you like, cut it off at the stem with a sharp knife, do a little dance and get cooking!

TIPS

Had enough of boiled cabbage? Give barbecued cabbage a try. Quarter and oil the cabbage, then barbecue until charred on all sides. It becomes really sweet and smoky, and is even better with a little cheese melted on top.

FRUIT

Achocha

Corn

Horned melon

Strawberries

Cucamelons

Pumpkins & Squashes

Peas

Tomatoes

Cucumber

Aubergine

Runner beans

Peppers & Chillies

Melons

French beans

ACHOCHA

Also known as a 'slipper gourd' or 'stuffing cucumber', I don't blame you if you haven't heard of this, let alone know how to pronounce its name. Just sound out 'ah-coach-ah' and you're pretty much there. This is one of those unusual vegetables that not only looks strange but tastes pretty good as well. They are a climbing vine that can reach up to 3m (10ft) high in perfect conditions and produce an abundance of medium-sized green pods with little soft spikes all over them. These pods can be eaten raw, but I prefer them cut up and fried – they taste a lot like green peppers. These peculiar pods are native to the Andes, but have been grown across Mexico, South America and Central America for hundreds of years. If you're looking for a weird vegetable that will happily grow outside along a railing or wall, then this is the one to try.

What you'll need:

- 8cm (3in) pots
- Multipurpose compost
- Achocha seeds (I like Fat Baby or Lady's Slipper)
- A container with at least a 20L (5.25 US gal) capacity

SOW

You only want to sow one to three seeds, otherwise you'll get too overwhelmed with plants. From early spring you can start your exotic quest and fill some 8cm (3in) pots to the top with compost. Make a hole in the centre of each pot with a pencil, finger or dibber that's 2cm (¾in) deep. Pop one seed in each hole and cover with a little more compost. Give them a decent water and keep them nice and warm on a windowsill.

GROW

Once they've germinated, keep them watered and happy in a sunny spot until they are around 12–15cm (5–6in) tall. You can now plant them outside, one plant per 20L (5.25 US gal) container. Fill your container almost to the top with compost, make a small hole in the centre and pop in one of your plants. If you're planting multiple plants into a larger container ensure that they're spaced 35cm (14in) apart. Give them some support that they can climb up, otherwise they'll just trail on the ground. Make any structure you like for them to climb up. You can create a wigwam with bamboo canes, a string or wire wall, or you can place them near an existing structure like some railings, a fence or even a washing line (see page 22). Keep them well watered. Finally, don't be alarmed by the maple-shaped leaves that appear once your plant gets going – you can assure your neighbours that it's definitely not cannabis!

GATHER

You'll have to wait till late summer before you can harvest the fruit. You can pick them when they are 'immature' (around 6cm/2½in for the Fat Baby variety) and the raw fruit will taste like cucumber. I prefer to let my fruit get a little more mature before I harvest it. I then remove the seeds (save a few for next year – see TIPS below) and treat them as I would bell peppers.

TIPS

Don't grow them inside unless you've got a castle or an empty greenhouse that needs filling. The frost in winter will kill them, so you don't need to worry about them taking over entirely. Be sure to remove any fallen fruit as they will readily self-seed anywhere they can.

CORN

If you could turn back time, I mean way back, like before Cher, you'd realize that corn was, in fact, not yellow at all. Corn was originally grown in the Americas and has been for around 10,000 years. Not only is it one of the most widely distributed crops in the world, it's actually got some of the most beautiful colours I've ever seen in a plant. I've grown lots of different types of corn over the years and although barbecued corn tastes great in any form, it's the rainbow cobs that steal the show. Most coloured varieties have to be used for flour or popcorn, as they are super starchy, but you can eat the young cobs at home before they become really vibrant.

What you'll need:

- Corn seeds (I love Double Red, Glass Gem and Incredible F1)
- Seed module tray, cardboard toilet roll tubes, or similar
- Multipurpose compost
- A raised bed, container or large pot (30L/8 US gal per 1–2 plants)

SOW

Sow corn seeds in mid-spring. Place a few sheets of kitchen paper on a clean surface and spritz with water. Place the corn seeds on the wet paper and cover with another sheet. Spritz again until everything is damp and put to one side for a couple of days, ensuring it stays damp. This helps the seeds to soften and speeds up germination. After two days, fill up your seed module tray with compost. With a pencil, finger or dibber, make a 2.5cm (1in) hole in the centre of each module and drop a seed in. Cover with a little more compost, water, then pop them in a warm, bright spot indoors.

GROW

Corn grows fast, so keep it damp and in a sunny spot. Once the plants are 15cm (6in) tall, fill your container with compost (you'll need a 30L/8 US gal pot per 1–2 plants), create small holes and pop a plant in each. If you're planting into a bed the seedlings need to be 10cm (4in) apart. Water well.

To ensure you get large cobs, you'll need to make sure your plants get plenty of 'action' (pollination). To do this, grow your plants in a block, rather than placing them in rows, so that pollen can pass from plant to plant as it falls.

GATHER

For standard sweet corn varieties, it's the general rule that once your cobs begin forming it will then take around six weeks for them to ripen. For other varieties, I often leave the cobs on the plants until early autumn. To test when they're ready, peel away the leaves at the top of a cob, press your nail into a kernel and it should squirt out a liquid – if this liquid is clear but slightly milky, then your corn is ready to harvest. The other method is to watch the silks that grow out of the top of the cob – once they turn brown they're ready. Twist and pull the cobs from the main stem in one swift motion.

TIPS

Give your plants a helping hand and shake their tassel tops when they look 'dusty' so the pollen falls all over the cob silks below and pollinates them. Corn can cross-pollinate with each other from up to a mile away, so if you grow more than one variety, then there's a chance they'll cross-pollinate and you'll end up with a mixed bag of coloured cobs.

If it's windy, tie your plants together. After all, there's safety in numbers.

HORNED MELON

Also known as 'Kiwano', 'Jelly Melon' or 'Spiked Melon', this is probably fruit you've never seen before, let alone tasted. With a flavour of grass and banana, some consider it to be the weirdest fruit they've ever eaten – I just think it's totally brilliant and something fun to grow at home. It originates from the Kalahari region in Africa where it can be seen growing wild. It's an annual climber that's related to melons and cucumbers, and it has small hairy leaves and extremely spiky fruit that begins green and ripens to a golden orange, with a radioactive-looking green jelly interior. They are such a peculiar fruit that they've even starred in various sci-fi films and TV series over the years as something you'd find growing on alien planets. Safety warning: overripe fruit will explode and fire seeds everywhere… but hopefully you'll pick them long before that happens. You'll need to grow them inside (or in a greenhouse or polytunnel) as they hate the cold. Interested in this alien fruit? Go buy some seeds then – they are available on Earth.

What you'll need:

- 8cm (3in) pots
- Multipurpose compost
- Horned Melon seeds
- A clear plastic bag big enough to cover your pot (like a freezer bag)
- A medium container (roughly 20L/5.25 US gal per 1–2 plants)
- Support so they can climb (string, railings, canes, etc)

SOW

Start sowing these tropical plants in mid-spring. Fill an 8cm (3in) pot to the top with compost, pull a single seed out of the packet and, holding it between your finger and thumb with the pointed end facing upwards, push it into the centre of the pot, about 1cm (½in) deep. Cover it with a little more compost, water gently and then cover the pot with a plastic bag and place it in a hot spot in your house (or in a propagator, if you have one). Repeat with any further seeds. You need the seeds to be in an atmosphere that's 21°C/70°F or more to germinate. You should see some action in 10 days or so.

GROW

Once your seeds have germinated remove the plastic bag. Keep your plants well watered and when they reach 10–13cm (4–5in) high pot them on in their final location. Fill up your chosen container with compost and make one or two small holes in the centre (well spaced if there are two). Place a seedling into each hole and secure with your hands. Push some bamboo canes into the soil next to your plants so that they have something to climb up and support them (they'll also climb along railings or bannisters). Don't let the horned melons dry out too much and give them a general feed if the leaves turn slightly yellow. Sit back and wait.

GATHER

If all has gone to plan, you'll have several fruits forming two to three months after sowing. They always seem to take forever to ripen, so you won't be harvesting until late summer or early autumn. Wait until they turn orange and soften slightly and they're ready for picking. Cut fruit from the vine using a sharp knife or scissors. I recommend wearing gloves, otherwise some expletives may escape your mouth when the melon spikes your hand. Cut it open, remove the seeds, and enjoy the jelly-like interior of this weird fruit – I promise it won't disappoint!

TIPS

Hand-pollination helps these wonderful fruits. Simply pick a flower from the plant, remove its petals, then rub the pollen-covered centre from flower to flower to spread the pollen.

STRAWBERRIES

Strawberries always remind me of my mum's obsession with British summer tennis tournaments and, when I was small, I'd devour them with both cream and ice cream – and then eventually feel a little sick!

Strawberries are actually big liars – in fact, they aren't a traditional fruit at all! They're actually a false fruit, which means the seeds (about 200 on each fruit) appear on the outside of the flesh rather than inside. As a planet we love strawberries, producing over 9 million tonnes of them each year, however, they haven't actually been around commercially for that long. The wild or alpine strawberry has been evident for hundreds of years, but it wasn't until the late eighteenth century that the garden strawberry was grown in France. You can now choose from lots of different varieties, including the very strange white strawberry. I don't advise growing strawberries from seed; instead buy them as small plug plants – it's not cheating and is a much faster way of getting to harvesting time. These fruits are really easy to grow and can yield a huge amount even in a tiny space.

What you'll need:

- Strawberry plug plants (I love Pineberry, Albion and Florence)
- Medium pot, hanging basket, raised bed
- Multipurpose compost
- General liquid feed

SOW

Buy your plug plants in mid-spring – they will either be in small pots or 'bare rooted' (meaning there will be little to no soil surrounding the roots). Whether they are naked or tucked up in a pot, I still treat them the same and plant them into their final container or basket straightaway. Fill your chosen container to the top with compost and then make some holes for each plant, 13–15cm (5–6in) apart. Pop a strawberry plant into each hole and secure the base of the plants with your hands. Place outside in a sunny spot and give them a water.

GROW

Your strawberry plants should grow fast and strong and begin to flower after a couple of months. I like to feed my plants every two weeks with a general liquid feed until the fruits begin to form. Watch out for slugs and snails and especially birds as they all love to eat strawberries. Put a net over your plants when the fruits begin to change colour and they should stay safe from those little peckers!

GATHER

Get that apron on, pick the fruits when they're rosy-red and let the jam making commence. The time of year for ripening strawberries will vary depending on the variety you chose, but you should get fruits over a four-week period in the summer, if not a little longer. Feel free to stuff your face with fresh strawberries, but not too many at once!

TIPS

If you want to save some cash and you know somebody who has some strawberry plants, go and ask if you can have the 'runners'. These are the side shoots that appear each year from established plants that you would normally remove. They can be cut off, potted up and then planted in your own garden. Do this to your own plants if you want even more strawberry plants growing in your garden next year.

CUCAMELONS

Is it a melon? Is it a cucumber? It's neither. Confused? I wasn't sure what to expect when I first set eyes on these grape-sized edible fruits a few years ago, but now I love them and grow several plants every year.

Also known as the 'mouse melon' or 'Mexican sour gherkin', and tasting like a cross between a cucumber and citrus fruit, cucamelons can be grown both indoors and outside, but tend to do better in warmer temperatures. They originate from Mexico (although a Mexican woman once told me she'd never seem them before and that I was a liar…!) and Central America, but it's only recently that they've become popular with growers and chefs.

Warning: you might not like the taste! This is due to the bitterness from the citrus flavour they have. Although most people enjoy the sharp twang, every so often someone is absolutely disgusted by them and how bitter they are. Bad luck if that's you; just leaves more for the rest of us.

What you'll need:

- Seed module tray or a small pot
- Multipurpose compost
- Cucamelon seeds (there's only one variety at the moment)
- A clear plastic bag big enough to fit your seed module tray or cover your small pot (like a freezer bag)
- A large container or raised bed

SOW

Sow cucamelons in early spring – they can be a bit slow to begin with. Fill up the seed module tray with compost right to the top, then use a pencil, finger or dibber to create two 1cm (½in) deep holes in each cell. Pop a seed in each hole and cover with a little more compost. I prefer to grow two plants together as they will ramble and cross over each other as they grow. Alternatively, fill a small pot with compost and sow your seeds into holes evenly spaced 1–2cm (¾in) apart. Water gently, then cover the seed module tray with a plastic bag (or place them in a propagator, if you have one). Keep them really hot for germination, something like 20–25°C (68–77°F) – a very sunny windowsill is best. They should germinate within 10 days – at this point, remove the plastic bag but keep them indoors and well watered but not soaked.

GROW

After about six weeks, a climbing shoot should grow from the centre of each plant – you can't miss this, as it's the main growing tip and it will be reaching to grab hold of anything nearby. Fill up your chosen container or bed with compost and also sort out some kind of supports for them to climb up (see page 22). Plant each pair of plants at the base of each support, you can help them climb with some careful wrapping/twisting. Place indoors or outside in a sunny spot, keep them watered and watch them grow... very slowly.

GATHER

Insects are very important for pollinating the fruit, so make sure they have access to your plants. Your plants should begin flowering and producing fruit after around 65 days from sowing. They're ready to pick when they're grape-sized, but are edible at any size. Eat them with fish, as a snack, or, my personal favourite, use them to garnish a G&T.

TIPS

If fruit is dropping before its fully formed then this is usually due to a lack of pollination and can be fixed with a bit of hand-pollinating. Simply pick a flower from the plant, remove its petals, then rub the pollen-covered centre from flower to flower.

PUMPKINS & SQUASHES

Cucurbits is the family name for gourds, squashes and pumpkins, which originate from Central America and have been eaten by humans for over 7,500 years. They are a rambling plant that grows predominantly along the ground and are great vegetables to grow with kids as they have massive seeds, are easy to look after and grow really fast. In fact, the current world record for a pumpkin is a ridiculous 1,190kg (2,624lb) – now that's something to aim for!

So say goodbye to the butternut, order some exciting squash seeds and prepare for an autumnal pumpkin party – there are so many fantastic shapes, colours and flavours to choose from!

What you'll need:

- 12cm (5in) pots
- Multipurpose compost
- Pumpkin or squash seeds (try Crown Prince, Jack Be Little, Atlantic
- Giant and Cornells Bush Delicata)
- Large pot, container or raised bed

SOW

In mid-spring, fill a 12cm (5in) pot to the top with compost, then pick a seed from the packet between your finger and thumb and, with the pointed end facing upwards, push it into the centre of the pot, about 2.5cm (1in) deep. Make sure that it is standing on its thin edge, as this will help prevent water sitting on the seed and rotting it. Repeat the process with however many seeds you'd like to sow, cover them with a thin layer of compost, water gently and pop them on a warm windowsill to germinate. Don't let them dry out.

GROW

After about three to four weeks the seedlings should have filled the pots with roots and be 8–12cm (3–5in) tall. At this stage, it's time to plant them into a larger container or bed. These plants are really fast growing and love to ramble everywhere, so it's best to grow them outside in a sunny spot. Fill your chosen container with compost and create small holes at 12cm (5in) intervals. If you can, place a lump of horse manure in the bottom of each hole. Pop a baby plant into each hole and secure by gently pressing down at the base with your hands. Keep them really well watered, as they like a good drink, and watch that pumpkin patch grow.

GATHER

Oh my gourdness, its autumn! Now, don't get twitchy and cut your prized squashes off prematurely. Let your plants die off to the point where all the leaves have turned brown and reveal all your lovely pumpkins. Frost can damage them so, before the first frost, cut each pumpkin/squash off the stem with a sharp knife, leaving 5cm (2in) of stem attached to the fruit. Give them a clean and let them dry and toughen up in a sunny spot for about a week. Then store them somewhere dark, dry and cool where they should keep for weeks, if not months (although this does vary depending on the variety). Now go stuff those squashes and carve that poor pumpkin.

TIPS

Although they won't climb like a vine, cucurbits can be trained to grow up a trellis or over an arch. That way you can maximize on your available space and lift your squashes off the ground in the process.

Feed will really help fruit development, especially if you've decided to grow a giant pumpkin. Feed once a week with tomato feed or liquid seaweed.

PEAS

Fresh peas taste awesome and are super easy to grow – you can even leave them in a wet bit of tissue and they'll be happy. If you're just after some pea shoots, then go check out the microgreens instructions on page 24, but here I'll show you how to achieve the real deal: mangetout and podded peas. Most commonly eaten from frozen or out of a can, peas are now grown across the world, having originated in the Mediterranean basin. Used prolifically throughout history, especially in times of famine as a source of fibre and protein, it wasn't until the seventeenth century in England that new varieties of the 'garden pea' were developed, and that eating them raw, rather than cooked, became popular. They grow not just with green pods but are also available in purples, yellows and some with a red/pink blush.

What you'll need:

- A small plastic tray
- A large container or grow bag that's 20L (5.25 US gal) or more
- Multipurpose compost
- Pea seeds (try Oregon or Magnolia)
- Support for your peas (see page 22)

SOW

You can sow peas anytime from early spring until midsummer. Line a plastic tray with kitchen paper or newspaper. Spritz with water so that it's damp and tip in the pea seeds. Cover with another layer of paper, spritz again, then pop the tray in a warm spot and don't let the seeds dry out. After three days most of the peas should have germinated and have little tails. Now they're ready to sow, so fill your chosen container or bed with compost. If you are sowing into a bed, use a trowel or your hand to create a long 10cm (4in) wide trench in the soil that's no more than 2.5cm (1in) deep. Pop a load of germinated seeds in (they can be touching or on top of each other, it really doesn't matter, just make sure they're packed in), then cover with a little more compost. If sowing into a pot, fill it with compost so it's about 5cm (2in) from the top, scatter the surface with germinated seeds and cover with another 2.5cm (1in) of compost. Water well and keep them in a sunny spot, preferably outside.

GROW

When you've got a good thick pea bush that's around 10cm (4in) high you will need to add some support. I prefer to use sticks or canes with string attached. Push the canes into the soil around your plants, then tie string between the canes to create a cage-like structure for your peas to climb up. If the leaves of your plants look a bit yellow near the base, then some general liquid feed will help give them a pick-me-up, especially later in the season in mid- to late summer. Keep watering daily.

GATHER

Most peas plants will be in full production 60 days from planting out. Harvesting times depend on the variety. If you want to eat the entire pod (like with sugar snap and mangetout), then pick the pods early when they're small and succulent – no more than 5cm (2in) long. If you're growing a variety to harvest the actual peas from inside the pod, you'll need to allow the pods to grow so that the peas have time to develop and get 'pea-sized' – prize open a pod to check. Be sure to keep picking, as the more you pick the more peas your plant will produce.

TIPS

If you have too many peas to get through, you can bag them up and pop them in the freezer as long as you intend to eat them within the next few weeks. If you want them to keep longer, blanch before freezing so you can dip into them right across the winter.

TOMATOES

I love the popping sensation as I bite into a delicious homegrown tomato, even though I inevitably squirt the juice onto my beard and down my top… If you take a look at the tomato family history it's filled with toxic and poisonous plants, yet somehow tomatoes have given up the family business of death and instead provide us with some great-tasting edible fruits. Originating from South and Central America, it wasn't until the Spanish discovered the Aztecs growing them that they were then introduced to Europe.

I can't stress how much better homegrown tomatoes are than the ones you get in the supermarket. Most commercially grown tomatoes either taste of nothing, or take on the flavour of the refrigerated lorry that they've travelled many miles in to get to your local store. Tomatoes aren't even supposed to be just red, but due to commercial demands, we've forgotten to appreciate all the other varieties with their wonderful patterns, shapes and colours.

Homegrown tomatoes taste and smell like nothing else. They can be grown indoors as well as outside and you don't need a lot of space to get an abundance of fruit. If you fancy trying some 'proper' tomatoes, then put down that punnet of watery toms and go order some seeds.

Some tomato varieties are climbers (the technical word for these varieties is 'indeterminate') and will need support while they grow in the form of canes or string. However, some varieties will happily grow as more of a bush or 'tumble' over the side of a container (these are 'determinate' varieties). Check the back of your seed packet to work out which you're growing.

What you'll need:

- 8cm (3in) pots
- Multipurpose compost
- Tomato seeds (try a mix of varieties, like Tigerella, Sungold, Bumble Bee and Orange Wellington)
- Plastic bag(s) large enough to cover your pots (like a freezer bag)
- Final location for your plants: hanging basket, grow bag, large pot, raised bed
- Support for your plants: string and bamboo canes (see page 22)

SOW

It's best to sow several tomato seeds in one pot (multi-sow) in early spring and then transplant them into bigger pots later on. Fill your small pot(s) with compost right to the top and then use a pencil, finger or dibber to poke 1cm (½in) deep holes spaced around 1cm (½in) apart across the compost surface. When you open your seed packet, you'll notice the seeds are a bit fiddly to handle, so carefully pop one seed in each hole and then cover. Water gently, cover the pot(s) with a plastic bag and pop them in a warm, bright spot like a windowsill (or put them in a propagator if you have one). Don't let them dry out.

GROW

In about a week, the seeds should have germinated. Remove the plastic bag once this happens, but keep them in their warm, bright spot. After a couple of weeks, you should have some decent-sized plants – 5–8cm (2–3in) tall – which means it is now time to 'split' them. Carefully tip the plants (compost and all) out of the pot(s) and begin to gently pull apart the individual plants. Gather more 8cm (3in) pots (as many as you have seedlings) and fill them right to the top with compost. Make a small hole in the centre of each pot and pop a baby tomato plant into each, so that each plant now has a pot to itself. Secure with your hands and a bit more compost if needed, then water well. Let them grow in a warm, bright spot until they are about 15cm (6in) high, at which point they'll be ready to move to their final container. You can plant into a raised bed, container or grow bag – each plant will need 25–30cm (10–12in) surrounding it, so choose a suitable container and have a think about how many plants you can fit in. It might be that you can only grow one per pot, depending on what containers you have to hand. Fill your chosen container with compost and make small holes in which to add your plants. Pop a plant in each hole and secure with your hands and a little more compost if needed. If you're using grow bags you just need to cut open the hole at the top and pop in your tomato plant. Depending on the size of your grow bag you may be able to fit two plants in each bag (a 30–40L/8–10.5 US gal growbag is roughly suitable for two tomato plants). Water well. If you're growing an indeterminate variety (see intro, opposite), then you need to add some support for your plants in the form of cane and string. Push the canes into the soil around your tomato plants, then tie string between the canes to create a cage-like structure for your tomatoes to climb up. Place your tomato plants in a warm, bright spot (indoors or outside) and keep them well watered. Once the plants begin flowering, start feeding them every two weeks with tomato food.

GATHER

Your tomatoes are ready for picking once they are plump and a little soft. Depending on what variety you've grown, it's hard to judge by colour, but most varieties start off green and ripen to orange, yellow, red, purple, or even remain green! Gently pluck off the plant or use scissors to snip them off at the stem. Enjoy the aroma of fresh tomato foliage and fruit, make yourself a fresh salad and never go back to buying supermarket tomatoes again.

TIPS

Did you know that tomato leaves are edible too? Use them to make pesto and add them to pasta or use them in a salad.

If you've got limited space, try growing a bush variety like Tumbling Tom or Cherry Cascade in a window box or hanging basket. Plant marigolds alongside your tomato plants to deter bad root nematodes and as a bonus you'll have some pretty flowers to look at.

Remove the leaves from the lower third of the plant once the fruits begin forming to ensure enough light reaches and ripens the tomatoes.

CUCUMBER

When it comes to growing cucumbers, there's not a lot I don't know. I'm renowned for my cucumber knowledge and you'll often find me waving these humble fruit about in summer. Do cucumbers grow well in your own country? The answer is probably yes, as they're found across the globe. Cucumbers originate from India and have been cultivated by humans for at least 3,000 years, although it was the Romans/Greeks who helped spread the cucumber love across Europe. It should come as no surprise that cucumbers come in all shapes, colours and sizes, rather than just the green, smooth and straight ones we buy in the supermarket. If you look after your cucumber plants well and give them support to climb everywhere you can easily enjoy fruit throughout summer and into early autumn.

What you'll need:
- 8cm (3in) pots
- Multipurpose compost
- Cucumber seeds (I love Dragon's Egg, Pony and Carmen)
- A final container or grow bag
- Support for your plants (see page 22)

SOW

Start sowing from early spring. Fill your 8cm (3in) pots to the top with compost. Hold one seed between your finger and thumb so that the pointed end is facing upwards. Push the seed into the centre of a pot so it's around 1cm (½in) below the surface, then cover it with compost. Repeat with more seeds, one per pot. Water gently, cover each pot with a plastic bag (or use a propagator) and pop them in a warm, bright spot. Don't let them dry out.

GROW

Let them grow until they have two sets of 'true leaves' – this means leaves with spiked edges, rather than the rounded seedling leaves that would have originally appeared on the plant after germination. At this stage they're ready to go into their final container. You can plant into a raised bed, container or grow bag – each plant will need 25–30cm (10–12in) surrounding it. It might be that you can only grow one per pot, which is fine. Fill your chosen container with compost and make small holes in which to add your plants. Pop a plant in each hole and secure with your hands and a little more compost if needed. If you're using grow bags you just need to cut open the hole at the top and pop in your cucumber plant. Depending on the size of your grow bag you may be able to fit two plants in each bag (a 30–40L/8–10.5 US gal growbag is roughly suitable for two cucumber plants). Water well. Push canes into the soil around your plants, then tie string between the canes to create a cage-like structure for them to climb up. Pop them in a warm, bright spot (indoors or outside) and keep them well watered. You can feed them every two weeks with a general liquid feed.

GATHER

Help your plants out by carefully tying them to the supports as fruit form and removing any leaves that turn yellow and die. You can harvest cucumbers at any size – the small ones are great for pickling, but you might want to wait until they've grown a little bigger so that you get more return on your efforts.

TIPS

If you have too many male flowers, they will cause your cucumbers to taste bitter. A male flower is obvious to spot, as it won't have any little fruits growing behind it. Simply pinch off and discard these flowers.

AUBERGINE (EGGPLANT)

Right, let's get one thing straight. It doesn't look like an egg, taste like an egg and it certainly didn't get pushed out a chicken's bottom. So where did the name 'eggplant' come from? Well, it actually stemmed from a small, white, egg-shaped variety of aubergine that was once very common in the eighteenth and nineteenth centuries across North America and Australia. It seems since then we've become accustomed to consuming mainly purple varieties, but they actually come in all manner of colours and shapes – some are even stripy!

Aubergines are part of the nightshade family (just like tomatoes, potatoes and peppers) and originate from Sri Lanka and India where they're used to absorb oils and spices in all sorts of incredible dishes.

What you'll need:

- 8cm (3in) pots
- Multipurpose compost
- Aubergine seeds (I love Striped Tonga and Ping Tung)
- A large pot or container (20L/5.25 US gal minimum per plant)
- Support for your plants (see page 22)

SOW

Although you want to start sowing in early spring, keeping aubergines warm at all times is key to getting big healthy plants. We need to multi-sow them first, so fill a small pot(s) with compost right to the top and use a pencil, finger or dibber to poke 1cm (½in)-deep holes spaced around 1cm (½in) apart across the compost surface. Carefully pop one seed into each hole, then cover the holes. Water gently, cover the pot(s) with a plastic bag and pop them in a warm, bright spot like a windowsill (or a propagator if you have one). Don't let them dry out.

GROW

After a few days the seeds should germinate – once this starts happening, remove the bag from the pot, but leave the plants in a sunny spot. When the seedlings are 3–4cm (1–1½in) tall it's time to 'split' them. Carefully tip the plants (compost and all) out of the pot(s) and gently pull apart the individual plants. Gather as many 8cm (3in) pots as you have seedlings and fill them right to the top with compost. Make a small hole in the centre of each pot and pop a seedling in so that each plant now has a pot to itself. Secure with your hands and more compost if needed, then water well. Let them grow in a warm,

bright spot inside until late spring – by this point their roots should have filled the pots. Fill some large containers with compost and make a small hole in the centre of each. Pop an aubergine plant into each hole, secure in place and water well. Push canes into the soil around your plants, then tie string between the canes to create a cage-like structure for them to climb up. For best results keep indoors in a warm, sunny spot (or in a greenhouse if you have one). They will manage outside if you have a south-facing garden or balcony, but like to be above 15°C (60°F). Keep them watered and give them a general liquid feed every two weeks once flowers appear.

GATHER

It takes an aubergine plant around four to five months from being sown to producing fruit. When they've reached a size you like and the skins are glossy use a sharp knife to cut them off at the stem. Don't let them get too big as they will become bitter.

TIPS

Aubergines benefit from hand-pollination. To do this rub a tiny paintbrush on the pollen-covered centre of each flower. You will transfer the pollen from flower to flower and help your plant procreate.

RUNNER BEANS

Also known as 'Scarlett runner bean' or 'multi flora', this is the bean that keeps on giving, sometimes even when you want it to stop. As a child growing up in a vegetarian household, the runner bean was a staple and there was no escaping them; even in winter they would make an appearance from the freezer.

Runner beans are one of the simplest beans to grow and they will literally thrive anywhere – indoors and out. They originate from the mountains of Central America, producing red flowers then large green pods filled with colourful beans and can grow over 2.8m (9ft) tall! If you'd like to have a bean forest of your own, teach your children about Jack and the Beanstalk and annoy your neighbours with endless bean giveaways, then give this plant a try.

What you'll need:

- 8cm (3in) pots or toilet roll tubes
- Multipurpose compost
- Runner bean seeds (try Scarlett Emperor or Polestar)
- Raised bed or large container
- Support for your plants (see page 22)

SOW

Sow in early to mid-spring. Fill up some 8cm (3in) pots (or toilet roll tubes) with compost and make two evenly spaced holes in the centre of each pot, about 2.5cm (1in) deep. Pop one seed into each hole – try to make sure they're standing up vertically. Cover with a little more compost, water well and pop on a warm windowsill. Don't let them dry out.

GROW

Keep those beans happy and watered until they start to produce a growing tip. Now they are ready to climb (very high) and you need to plant them out into their final spot. Fill a raised bed or large container with compost and use a trowel or your hands to create small holes 20cm (8in) apart. Pop a baby runner bean plant into each hole, secure with your hands and give them a water. Push canes into the soil around your plants, then tie string between the canes to create a cage-like structure for them to climb up. You can also tie netting between the canes for even more support and they'll happily climb along banisters or balcony railings. You can grow runners inside if you have enough light, but they'll enjoy being outside in the sunshine. Keep them watered, but not soaked, and watch them climb.

GATHER

Once the plants start to flower, you should be drowning in runner beans by early summer. The more you pick, the more will grow, and I recommend harvesting them when they're still anywhere under 10 inches – the bigger they get the tougher they become. Just pull or snip them off the plant as and when they come. Be careful when picking the beans off the plants that you don't damage any of the smaller beans before they're ready to harvest.

TIPS

If you'd like to ensure a bean-filled winter, then pick, slice, blanch, bag and freeze your glut of beans throughout the summer.

Watch out for wind! No, I don't mean the side-effect of mass runner bean consumption (although watch out for that too…). Your bean plants can get blown over and damaged on a breezy day, so take the time to tie them onto your canes and/or netting with string as they grow.

PEPPERS & CHILLIES

Most supermarkets only offer a fairly boring selection of bell, jalapeño and cayenne peppers, but there are so many varieties out there in numerous shapes, sizes and colours and ranging from sweetness to the hottest of chilli. One of my favourites is a pepper called Black Knight that is almost black in colour – it looks brilliant in a salad, but interestingly loses its colour when roasted.

Peppers originate from South America and have been consumed by the human race for thousands of years, but it wasn't until the colonization of the Americas that peppers became common across Europe and Asia. Spanish and Portuguese traders finally had a spice to offer that was different to black pepper, and the chilli pepper spread like wildfire. It wasn't until the 1920s that the sweeter bell pepper was developed.

What you'll need:

- 8cm (3in) pots
- Multipurpose compost
- Pepper seeds (I love Joe's Long, Black Knight, Candy Cane and Sweet Heat)
- A final container for them to grow in (20–30L/5.25–8 US gal per plant)

SOW

Peppers take a while to grow, so starting them off in early spring is important. Fill an 8cm (3in) pot with compost almost to the top. Use a pencil or small dibber (not your finger this time) to poke four evenly spaced holes into the surface of your pot, 1cm (½in) deep. Pop one seed in each hole, cover with a little more compost and give them a gentle water. Leave your plants on a warm windowsill with a plastic bag over the top (or in a propagator) – they like to be around 20°C (68°F). Don't let them dry out.

GROW

Once your pepper seedlings are big enough to handle (6cm/2½in tall), it's time to 'split' them. Carefully tip the plants (compost and all) out of the pot and gently pull apart the individual plants. Gather as many 8cm (3in) pots as you have seedlings and fill them with compost. Make a small hole in the centre of each pot and pop a seedling in, so that each plant now has a pot to itself. Secure with your hands and more compost if needed. Let them grow in a warm, bright spot inside and keep them well watered but not soaked. Once they have doubled in size (12cm/5in tall) transfer them to a large container, 20–30L (5.25–8 US gal) pot per plant.

Fill your containers with compost, use a trowel or your hands to make a small hole in the centre of each, then pop a pepper plant into each hole. Secure well and give them a water. The more heat they get the better, so keep them indoors by a sunny window, in a south-facing spot outside, or in a greenhouse.

GATHER

If you've grown a sweet pepper you can pick them at any stage – allow them to get to a size you like, then cut them off at the stem with a sharp knife. With chilli peppers it's a little different – you want them to change colour and mature before harvesting them. Safety warning: if you're growing a chilli variety, then please wash your hands after handling both the leaves and fruit, and even then, avoid touching your face or delicate areas. It's best to harvest hot chilli peppers while wearing rubber gloves.

TIPS

If your pepper plant is being weighed down by its own fruit, push a cane into the soil and then gently tie the stems to it with string. For a bumper crop pinch out the growing tips (the very top bit of the plant) and give your plants a general liquid feed every couple of weeks.

MELONS

The first time I managed to grow a melon (in the UK), I was a surprised by how easy it was. I was even more surprised when nobody believed that I'd grown it. This seems to be a common theme in countries that don't traditionally grow melons, but whether you want a sweet cantaloupe or chunky watermelon, all you need is heat. These sweet fruiting climbers were one of the first plants to be domesticated and grown by humans, and they originate from the hotter climates of Africa and the hot valleys of southwest Asia. Melons love a good ramble and will climb vertically as well as sprawl along the floor – they seem happy doing either. To grow melons at home it's best if you have a hot indoor space in which to put them, like a warm room or greenhouse, but you can also create a 'mini tunnel' over a raised bed or pot outside using purpose-made metal hoops, clear plastic (you can buy these online or from a plant centre) and a few stones to keep things secure.

What you'll need:

- 8cm (3in) pots
- Multipurpose compost
- Melon seeds (I like the watermelon Sugar Baby and the cantaloupe Minnesota Midget
- Plastic bag(s)
- Large container or raised bed
- Support for your plants (see page 22)

SOW

Sow in early spring. Fill your 8cm (3in) pots with compost and compact it down a little. Hold a seed between your finger and thumb with the pointed end facing upwards. Push the seed into the centre of a pot so it's around 1.5cm (¾in) below the surface, then cover it with compost. Repeat with more seeds, one per pot, depending on how many plants you'd like to grow. Water gently, place a plastic bag over the top of each pot and pop them in a warm, bright spot (or in a propagator) – they need to be at least 22°C (72°F) to germinate. Don't let them dry out.

GROW

Once they have germinated remove the plastic bags. Keep them watered and let them grow to 10–15cm (4–6in) high with plenty of leaves. In early summer, fill up your large container or raised bed with compost and use a trowel or your hands to make small holes 20cm (8in) apart. Pop a baby melon plant into each hole, secure with your hands, then give them a good water. Push canes into the soil around your plants, then tie string between the canes to create a cage-like structure for them to climb up. Place them in a very sunny spot – a greenhouse if you have one – keep them warm and wait for flowers. You can grow them inside your house as long as they have plenty of natural light. Insects will pollinate the flowers, but if you're growing the plants indoors, then you'll need to do some hand-pollinating. To do this, find a male flower (it's the one that's hasn't got a little melon growing behind it). Gently break away the petals – you'll see that the centre is covered in pollen. Rub this pollen-covered centre on the centre of each female flower (the ones with little melons growing behind them). And that's it – hand-pollination complete. Reduce the amount you water them once fruit begins to form. Feeding the plants once a week with a general liquid feed or tomato feed will give them a helping hand.

GATHER

If you've grown watermelons, keep an eye on the closest curly tendril to the fruit. Once this turns brown your watermelons are ready to harvest.

For all other melons it's best to go by smell. Pick up a melon and give the bottom of it a sniff – if it smells strongly of sweet melon, then it's ripe and ready to harvest. Colour change does happen, but I find this happens when they are becoming overripe.

FRENCH BEANS

Green beans, squeaky beans, bush beans, stringless beans. Whatever you call them everybody remembers chewing on boiled beans as a kid and hearing that small mouse squeaking away in their mouth. When it comes to French beans you can get two types; dwarf and climbing. There's actually nothing particularly French about these beans. The name occurs because, having originated in South America, they became readily available across Europe in the nineteenth century and were extremely popular in France where they were (and still are) called 'haricots verts'.

Commonly only green varieties are grown commercially, but there are also purple and yellow varieties available, both in dwarf and climbing forms. If you've got a bare bannister, balcony railing or wall you'd like to fill, then give these guys a try as they will climb up anything given the chance.

What you'll need:

- 8cm (3in) pots or toilet roll tubes
- Multipurpose compost
- French bean seeds (Sunshine, Amethyst and Sprite are great)
- A final raised bed, pot or container (30L/ 8 US gal per plant)
- Support for your plants (see page 22)

SOW

Sow your beans in mid-spring. Fill your small pots or cardboard tubes with compost and compact it in a little. Poke a finger-sized hole in the centre of each pot, about 2.5cm (1in) deep. Drop a seed into each hole, cover with a little more compost, give them a water and pop them on a warm windowsill.

GROW

Ensure the bean plants get lots of sunlight and don't let them dry out too much. Once your baby bean plants are bushy, climbing tendrils are beginning to show and they have filled their pots with roots, it's time to pot them on. Fill a large container or raised bed with compost and use a trowel or your hands to create small holes roughly 15cm (6in) apart.

For dwarf plants, pop one plant into each hole and secure it with your hands. For climbing plants, add two plants to each hole (this is so that two plants can climb up the same support). Give them a good water.

If growing climbing beans, push canes into the soil around your runner bean plants, then tie string between the canes to create a cage-like structure for them to climb up. You can also tie netting between the canes for even more support, and they'll happily climb along banisters or balcony railings – think about what you have available and adjust accordingly.

Place them in a warm, bright spot indoors or outside and keep them watered.

GATHER

After around 12 weeks from sowing you should be able to start picking beans from your plants – they should be 10–13cm (4–5in) long. Carefully pull the beans off the plants (no need for scissors). The more you pick, the more will appear!

TIPS

Climbing beans will grow up anything, so get inventive and work with what you have. String, wire, wooden frames, bamboo and, my old favourite, nets! Dwarf French beans can yield just as many fruits as climbing varieties and are perfect grouped near each other in individual pots.

Index

S

Sam Corfield (aka The Hairy Horticulturist) is a trained horticulturist, cameraman and expert vegetable grower residing in Cornwall, South West England. Having spent many years working and training at the world-renowned Lost Gardens of Heligan, Sam now has a large online following on Instagram, where he provides information and education on growing-your-own and self-sufficiency. His work has led to him building a large kitchen garden for an award-winning pub, managing a five-acre farm shop vegetable garden and growing an impressive beard. Sam loves to grow more unusual varieties of fruit and veg that you wouldn't find in your local shop or supermarket and encourages his fans to do the same with his unique, fun and accessible approach to gardening. He is currently renovating a 750-year-old mill where he hopes to grow vegetables for many happy years to come. This is his first book.

Come say hi: @the_hairy_horticulturist

To all the vegetables that have made the ultimate sacrifice over the years, I thank you!

Working in horticulture isn't an easy path to take in life and to really understand it and learn your craft takes years of monotonous tasks that you repeat season after season. However, it's something I love, that's become part of me, that's crafted me into this bearded vegetable-waving weirdo and I'm lucky enough to call it work.

Firstly, I'd like to thank my partner Sarah, you've always been there for me, even when we've been apart. Thank you to my parents and grandparents for your endless support and love, you've all taught me so much both in life and in the garden.

Thank you to my editor Harriet Webster, for your guidance, support and advice. You've taken the vegetable ramblings I've put before you and made them into something rather lovely.

Thank you to Dave Brown, someone I'm now lucky enough to call my friend. You've designed such a beautiful book, taken such wonderful photos and put up with my endless 'porn poses'.

Thank you to Quadrille for allowing me this opportunity to create something rather special, if not different.

Thanks to Reuben, Charlie, Emily and Darcy for allowing me to build such a large garden and grow a disgusting number of vegetables at your house.

Many thanks to Tanya and Alex – you let me build, grow and create a beautiful and productive kitchen garden at your pub, I'm forever grateful.

Thanks to Jim, James and Dr Tony, you all taught me so much, some of which I didn't need to know!

Thank you to specialist wildlife cameraman Ian Llewellyn, for all you've taught me over the years both in wildlife and in life. More recently I've loved our fun-filled, albeit slightly weird, vegetable work together. I wouldn't be half as strange as I am without you!

Thank you to all those I've worked with, that have shared their knowledge and ideas with me.

Finally, thanks to those that have given their lives to the garden, I miss them dearly.

Pard, the tide waits for no man!

Publishing Director
Sarah Lavelle

Commissioning Editor
Harriet Webster

Head of Design
Claire Rochford

Art Direction & Design
Dave Brown

Photographer
Dave Brown

Head of Production
Stephen Lang

Production Controller
Sabeena Atchia

First published in 2022
by Quadrille, an imprint
of Hardie Grant
Publishing

Quadrille
52–54 Southwark Street
London SE1 1UN
quadrille.com

The rights of Sam Corfield to be
identified as the author of this work
have been asserted by him in
accordance with the Copyright,
Design and Patents Act 1988.
Cataloguing in Publication Data:
a catalogue record for this book is
available from the British Library.

ISBN: 978 1 78713 716 5

Printed in China

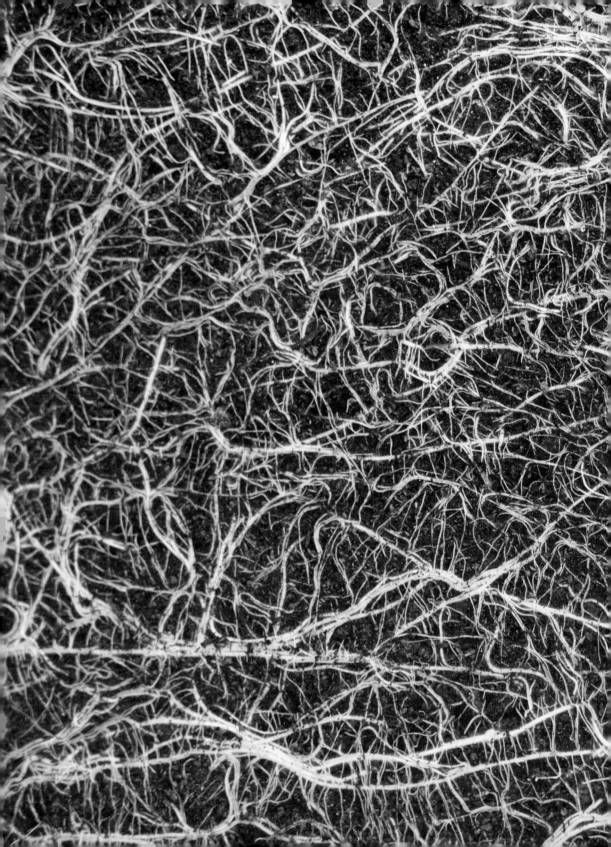